DISCARDED

P

Making Your Sc

D1488751

"Wow! Rushton Hurley presents a passionate and powerful message for all educators in this book that gets to the heart and soul of what teaching is all about! My imagination was stirred by what's possible in our schools today! A must-read for anyone in the profession who wants to make a difference!"

—**Dr. Kathy Perez**, Professor of Education,
Saint Mary's College of California

"Building school culture and creating a positive climate is crucial for student success. Having the capacity to collaborate and create as educators only helps to improve the environment for the students we serve. In this book, Rushton lays out some simple ways any school can make it a place where innovation, imagination, and excellence flourish. It's one you'll want to revisit over and over again to keep improving!"

—**Steven W. Anderson**, Educational
Evangelist and Speaker/Consultant

"What a great read! I kept switching my past and present hats paragraph by paragraph, wishing I had understood so many of the concepts earlier in my teaching career and in the sixteen years I have been supporting teachers as a principal and superintendent. Each chapter flows into the next, acting as motivation to keep learning and maintain engagement. At the heart of the book, and mentioned early, is the belief that digital media can't compete with the power of a strong teacher. This very true statement opens the door to many successful potentially motivating dialogues with all teachers, honoring and giving hope to all those looking to make learning special for kids."

—**Aubrey Patterson**, Superintendent, Lloydminster Catholic School Division, Lloydminster, Alberta, Canada

"*Making Your School Something Special* offers wonderful insights for classroom teachers—insights that can lead teachers to not only reflect upon and improve learning experiences for their students, but also cultivate a culture of collaboration and creativity where cool ideas and projects are shared and celebrated."

—**Dennis Grice**, Digital Literacy Instructional Coach, Concordia International School Shanghai

"*Making your School Something Special* is simply an excellent resource for educators. Rushton accomplishes a deft feat—providing inspiration while keeping feet solidly planted on the ground, respecting educators while challenging them to more, recognizing the intrinsic desire of students to engage their learning while accepting their limitations—in the end providing inspiring and concrete ideas on how to change the culture of your school to embrace students, community and the highest ideals we have for learning. Rushton's ideas reflect his love of learning and his deep knowledge of school life and teachers. His inspiration and enthusiasm for learning are contagious!"

—**Barry Thornton**, Principal, Junipero Serra High School

"Over the last decade I have listened to Rushton Hurley speak at education conferences across this country. I was consistently impressed with his intelligence, humor, vast amount of knowledge, and ability to inspire. I always found myself wanting hear more after each engagement. This book fills that need with a fresh approach to student-centered education that could and should infuse the culture of every school."

—**Tom Whitby**, author, blogger, speaker,
podcaster, consultant, 40-year educator,
Lollapalooza Consultant Group

"When I pick up a to-do-with-work book, the temptation is to skim read, pick out a couple of bits, check out the bullet points, have a think, job done, move on. But this is a beginning-to-the-end kind of book. It's not too long, so find some time, sit down with it, and relish the story.

"There's a fair few examples of using technology—no surprise, given Rushton's background. It also does what, deep down, you expect: leaves you to work out for yourself how to make your school something special.

"Tying the book closely to practice, and only loosely to theories or systems, makes it engaging and leaves it packed with transferable learning for teachers from schools with any age children, from any country, in any education system."

—**Marcus Belben**, Elearning and Multimedia Manager,
University of Birmingham, Birmingham, United Kingdom

"I have had the good fortune to see Rushton speak a few times over the last handful of years, and the thing I appreciate about him is that he talks with teachers and not at them. I am pleased that this voice is also apparent through the words in his book. His varied background in education instills in him the authority to share ideas that every teacher should hear and be open to.

"Rushton is a masterful storyteller. He weaves in stories from his own adventures that help to tell a story or prove a point on what he believes is crucial in an effective learning environment. As an educator first, technology integrator second, I appreciate that his book does not preach to 'try this new thing with technology' or to 'try out this new app or website.' The broadcast is to be open while crafting your own something special. These stories and challenges will meet all levels of need—from the new teacher just deciding what path to head out onto, the teacher that's been in the game a little while, to the veteran who feels as if he or she has seen it all. This is a great read to validate that you, as an educator, do have that something special. It will inspire you to continually find new ways to broadcast your message.

—**Chad Kafka**, Tech Integration Specialist for Franklin Public Schools, Wisconsin

"In this little book, Rushton Hurley has described what a school can become when teachers engage students in challenging and meaningful work and when schools enable teachers to work together to build upon successes.

"The highly readable and engaging book consists mainly of brief stories drawn from the author's years working with schools in the nonprofit he founded, Next Vista for Learning, helping schools, teachers, and students to improve. These stories illustrate a few powerful principles the author has identified from the successes he has seen and fostered in his work with schools, principles, such as memorable learning experiences; sharing and building on successes; collaboratively exploring new possibilities; and sustaining confidence and effort.

"Although he doesn't make such a claim, the vision he outlines here could go a long way toward realizing the schools we need for the twenty-first century—not a backward-looking focus on excellence at purely academic tasks, and not a do-your-own-thing student-centered progressive vision, but a focus on tackling exciting and meaningful challenges with teamwork and collaboration. These are the very qualities the next generation needs in order to thrive in a dynamic gig economy that demands and rewards innovation and initiative. I highly recommend this book to teachers, principals, and anyone concerned about the state of elementary and secondary education today."

—**Decker Walker**, Emeritus Professor, Graduate
School of Education, Stanford University

"In *Making Your School Something Special*, Rushton Hurley weaves memorable stories and anecdotes with practical advice so that we can all level up our games. He talks about four types of school activities: the powerfully memorable, the generally effective, the weak but easy, the waste of time.

"Which of the things that you normally do fall within each category? How much more enjoyable would your experience be if you operated consistently in the powerfully memorable or generally effective? How much more engaged would your students be?

"*Making your School Something Special* guides you so that you are routinely performing generally effective or powerfully memorable activities. This book has the potential to transform schools."

—**Mitch Weisburgh**, co-Founder,
Academic Business Advisors

"If you're reading this then you're someone who believes, like Rushton Hurley, that school can be a better place for teaching and learning. *Making Your School Something Special* describes school environments to which we can all relate. Whether to better celebrate positive outcomes already happening or finding ways to improve the current circumstances, teachers, administrators, staff, and parents will find creative and inspiring ways to change their school from good enough to something special. Rushton writes with great wit and thoughtful insight that makes you laugh out loud and think introspectively, often at the same time! Like a good coffee-shop conversation with a friend, his stories are filled with examples and insights gleaned from schools around the world, and yet seemingly tailored to your situation. Read it with colleagues and build your own stories that inspire you to find ways you all agree, 'My school is special because....'"

—**Steven J. McGriff**, Ph.D., Founder,
DivergentED Consultants

Making Your School Something SPECIAL

by Rushton Hurley

Making Your School Something Special
© 2016 by Rushton Hurley

These books are available at special discounts when purchased in quantity for use as premiums, promotions, fundraising, and educational use. For inquiries and details, contact the publisher: edtechteam.com/press.

Published by EdTechTeam Press
Cover design by Genesis Kohler
Editing and Interior Design by My Writers' Connection

Paperback ISBN: 978-1-945167-27-0
eBook ISBN: 978-1-945167-28-7
LCCN: 2017931416

Irvine, California

Contents

Preface

The chances are good you are holding this book because you work at or with a school, you believe in the possibilities of the school's community, and you want that school to reach its potential. Another strong possibility is that you were assigned this book as part of a teacher pre-service program, and you realize that what you bring to your professional team requires more than instructional talent.

You may be reading this as part of an organizational management class and believe that the kind of team-building strategies and thinking that inspires young people can also bring the best out of teams in other settings.

And though unlikely, it is also mathematically possible that you lost a bet and are now reading this book to pay your debt to the winner.

Whatever your reason for taking on the topic of building a great community, thank you.

Why the gratitude? Well, for one, a portion of the proceeds from this book's sales will support the efforts of Next Vista for Learning, the educational nonprofit organization I founded in 2005. Next Vista works to highlight creative approaches to teaching and learning, with its principal effort a free library of videos by and for teachers and students everywhere. I am regularly impressed by the insightful approaches to sharing stories of learning that we find in these videos, so I appreciate that you are helping with this effort.

At a much higher level, however, thank you for wanting to inspire students to see their world from new perspectives. I believe that anyone working to make a school a place of creativity, excellence, imagination, distinction, and professional exploration is necessarily shaping new avenues for students—avenues that can lead them to see their possibilities in wonderful ways.

For most teachers, gratitude is most keenly felt from seeing students realize that they are capable of more than they had imagined. A strong rapport and clever encouragement have always made for great moments professionally. What is new, though, is the variety of tools, resources, and ideas great teachers are harnessing to extend their professional talents to reach students who have had trouble in more traditional settings.

Looking at what is now possible, I would contend that there has never been a better time to teach.

I know that may sound a bit odd—it's not as if teaching is a well-respected position in the United States and many other parts of the world. In fact, countries that adequately compensate and highly regard their teachers are the exception, not the rule.

That said, several challenges facing teachers in the past have either lessened considerably, or disappeared altogether.

Among them is what I would call the cancer of our profession: isolation. Not too long ago, it wasn't uncommon for teachers to have remarkably few intellectually stimulating conversations over the course of the school year. One could be the only teacher for a subject or grade level, leaving no one to turn to for immediately useful ideas for lessons. One could have plenty of colleagues, but none of them might hold the same interest and/or passion that drives the need to experiment.

Thanks to modern technology, you can reach out to colleagues teaching the same subject or grade level at any time and connect with those excited to see what a new idea can do. You discover that not only are you *not alone*, but that there are many others who share the same quirky interests and face the same kinds of unusual challenges.

We're also living in a time when interesting tools and helpful articles and videos aren't limited to a few publishing and media entities; rather, the pendulum has swung wildly to the other extreme, with fascinating possibilities continuously being shared, proposed, and documented—the vast majority being freely available. Navigating this ocean of ideas can be daunting, but compared to before, when finding anything of value could prove a challenge, I think this is a great problem to have.

What's more, this explosion of contacts and ideas has set in motion an even greater advantage: As more and more of us embrace these powerful changes, the possibilities increase rapidly for strengthened professional discussion and even heightened school morale.

This book is about how we, as educators and education supporters, can take advantage of this new world so that, together, we can enhance our students' learning experiences and at the same time strengthen teachers' professional and personal experiences.

Although many of the ideas I discuss will incorporate technology, by no means are they limited to schools with significant technological resources. Rather, I want to show that how we think about, explore, and pursue our possibilities can result in better outcomes across the board—including happier, more successful students, as well as a healthier more interesting work environment for those of us on the front lines.

My Background

So who is this "Rushton" guy, anyway? Is that even a real name?

It is. "Rushton" is my mother's maiden name, and it's been good fun having a given name that hardly anyone else on the planet has. I'll add that my mother is a dedicated and inspiring professor of English, and I grew up under the grammatical gun in an environment frequently peppered with wonderful references to great literature and poetry. Any errors in this book are certainly not her fault.

As to the first question, I am a former high school and college teacher of Japanese language, a former school principal, a former professional-development program designer and director, a current social benefit entrepreneur, and a guy lucky enough to travel the world sharing and exploring ideas on possibilities for teachers and schools.

Let's look at those items individually.

I should start by noting that in addition to Japanese, I spent a year team-teaching English at schools in Japan via the Japan Exchange and Teaching (JET) Program.[1] I spent the year after I graduated from college in the Goto Islands of Nagasaki Prefecture in far-western Japan, where I learned I really enjoyed working with the always-fascinating class of humanity known as teenagers.

I have also taught social studies courses, and even did a brief stint with a summer math program. Teaching a variety of subjects at different levels has allowed me to better understand what motivates students in different settings. I've spent the bulk of my time in the classroom teaching Japanese as an elective, though, as part of a career that has spanned more than twenty-five years in Japan, California, Texas, and even Western Australia.

As a principal in Texas, I spent a short time with a K–12 school before joining the state's 2001–2003 virtual schooling pilot program and becoming the principal of an online high school. I found this to be some of the most intellectually interesting work of my career as my team and I worked to craft a meaningful, challenging, and interesting curriculum using what was available online at the time. I had a truly wonderful and dedicated

---

[1] https://jetprogramusa.org

team of teachers, and I thoroughly enjoyed exploring how we could make online learning work for students who had been less-than-perfect matches for the traditional classroom.

Because of my experiences with teachers at many different levels in a variety of settings, I was given the opportunity to spend three years running a teacher professional development program at the Krause Center for Innovation (KCI) at Foothill College in Los Altos Hills, California. With its unique mix of ubiquitous technologies, unusual architecture, and excited educators, the KCI is one of the more interesting places on the planet, and the many talented teachers I have encountered through the KCI have helped me explore all sorts of possibilities I would otherwise have missed.

Back in 2005, I began working on an idea that would become the nonprofit I founded, Next Vista for Learning, an effort to collect short, creative insights on what students often find challenging in school. The impetus to make this organization my primary focus came via the generosity of my good friends from college, Steve and Rebecca, who convinced me not to put off giving the idea a shot.

Over the last ten years and change, I have watched Next Vista for Learning's website, NextVista.org, grow to house over two thousand videos submitted by teachers and students from every continent—other than, of course, the one far to the south that is melting too quickly. These videos help students and teachers gain new perspectives on a wealth of topics, including everyday school subjects, various careers, communities around the world, and the joy and meaning that come from helping others.

I run Next Vista for Learning almost completely using the revenue I earn from speaking and training at schools and conferences. Since I began keynoting conferences in 2008, I've shared creative approaches to learning and teaching with more than 100,000 teachers around the world. Many of these teachers and school leaders have shared with me all sorts of intriguing approaches for inspiring students, as well as powerfully effective ways to lead at schools.

Finally, there's that "travel the world" thing. I'm forever grateful to the wonderfully cool EdTechTeam people for giving me the opportunity to speak at dozens of events over the last four years. Meeting dynamic teachers working in a variety of educational settings, visiting their schools, listening to their stories, and being inspired by their efforts is a pretty sweet way to spend one's time.

Through these conversations in so many different settings, I've come to learn how schools can effectively foster a sense of personal and professional community while connecting with a variety of organizations— other schools near and far, nonprofits, and community-minded organizations and companies—to bring new opportunities to their learners.

It is to these people I owe thanks for the best ideas in this book. Every successful school finds ways to tap into the talents of its team, and gets these professionals to build new possibilities by sharing ideas regularly. I hope these suggestions will help you and your colleagues tap into one another's insights, along with enjoying the boundless wealth that can come from strengthening your students' creativity and talents.

May what you and they imagine result in a school that is for all of you—something truly special.

Chapter 1
The Question

Fairly often, the short line at the grocery store is definitely not the short line for me—when it comes to the time it takes to get through it. Perhaps the person at the front has picked up an item that the price reader doesn't recognize; or maybe the customer and clerk are properly skeptical that $48 is not, in fact, the right price for the box of breakfast cereal; or the crawl becomes a halt as a rather unusual customer attempts to barter with the tired teen behind the counter. Whatever the circumstances, being in a hurry greatly increases my chances of the universe organizing itself so that I get to observe the kerfuffle unfold in rather painful detail.

For our purposes, let's assume it is you, not me, in line, and it is you the universe has conspired against. Consider this situation as one that affords you the time to think about everything you still have on your to-do list that day as you glacially navigate the gauntlet of gossip literature and breath mints assaulting your vision from all angles.

Let's also assume that you work at a school, and on this day, behind you in line, are parents with a child who looks about the age of those who enter your place of employment each autumn.

You and the parents begin talking, and upon finding out where you work, they comment that your school is one of the ones they are considering for their kiddo, who has now directed her attention your way, realizing you may play some part in her future.

One of the parents then asks: "What makes your school special?"

What makes your school special?

So you think. There may be well-known strengths that the community celebrates. Students may pass down history from class to class, instilling a sense of pride in what it means to be a student or alum of your school.

Perhaps the school is loaded with programs and activities designed to identify and foster the strengths of children of all backgrounds and abilities. There may be some activity, effort, or opportunity that easily distinguishes your school, and that might make answering the parent's question easy.

Or you could give a fairly common answer that says nothing useful at all: "Well, we really care about our students."

Great. You have just cleanly differentiated your school from all those institutions of learning that specialize in traumatizing children however possible.

Answers reaching this level of blandness are more common than you might think. In some ways, it's a default response, along the lines of "Doin' good!" to "How you doin'?"

But why do we so often hear (and give) vague, uninteresting answers like this? As we dive into this book, we will explore both the background for such unhelpful responses, as well as how you and your colleagues can give far better answers to parents wanting to know what possibilities may await their children within the walls of your school.

Chapter 2
Speaking of 'Special'

Any number of adjectives could describe the type of school I want to help foster through writing this book, including "good," "strong," "exceptional," "remarkable," and "successful." For our purposes, though, we will focus on the idea of "special" as a way to suggest:

- The experiences of both the students and teachers are individually meaningful and inspiring.

- The school's community of learners and educators explores and crafts that which creates shared affection and pride.

- Genuinely distinctive opportunities to develop academically and grow personally are available to everyone.

To create such a school, a team should have a clear understanding of and focus on its overarching goals, so

I want to offer three such goals to frame my approach to a school's improvement:

First, students must have memorable learning experiences, and have them regularly. Making learning memorable requires taking activities that merely move students through the curriculum and turning them into unpredictable moments of intrigue and excitement. Doing this requires us to know where our true successes lie and when to build upon them. In that same vein, we must also be honest about what doesn't measure up, and constantly adjust our course in pursuit of powerfully effective activities to serve the variety of students in the class.

In "Chapter 3: Learning Successes," we'll examine what makes learning memorable and identify types of learning activities, ranging from amazing to miserable.

Second, the adults who work at the school (teachers, librarians, administrators, technologists, coaches, counselors, aides, clerical staff, bus drivers, meal preparers—everyone who helps guide and arrange students' experiences) should work together to pursue an exploratory culture. We all can and should contribute ideas that can lead to successes, and we can and should work together to build and improve upon these learning stories so that the community can share them beyond our campuses.

In "Chapter 4: Exploratory Culture," we'll identify what makes for constructive professional interaction, how a team can use time well to generate memorable learning experiences, and why sharing success stories within and beyond the team is a fundamental piece of making this all work.

Third, everyone working at a school should help students develop their individual confidence as well as address the adults' need to become confident professionals. From avoiding reinventing the wheel, to showing a willingness to learn from students, to using technology to change fundamental pieces of the classroom experience, there is a world of approaches that can result in new ways of thinking about our abilities.

In "Chapter 5: Individual Confidence," we'll look at ideas for bringing what we do to higher levels and helping students see themselves as capable learners.

Technology's Role

You'll notice that as I continue building my case for fostering improvement within our schools, I will regularly draw attention to the role technology can play in making a school something special.

I should note from the outset that technology's role in this pursuit is less about the concrete forms it takes (e.g., the devices, sites, programs, apps, and tools) and more about how it shapes possibilities for us and our students. After all, the point of departure for significant successes is often how we perceive technology. A common mistake teachers make, though, is thinking their experience with technology falls along a single spectrum: either you're good with tech or you aren't.

> Technology's role in this pursuit is less about the concrete forms it takes and more about how it shapes possibilities for us and our students.

While there are certainly those of us more familiar with various technologies than others, at core, we all have the capacity to ask useful questions and imagine possibilities. Strong, thoughtful questions are what allow us all to explore interesting possibilities with technologies. In fact, prior knowledge and experience can actually make it more difficult to see creative new avenues for learning through either traditional or cutting-edge tools.

Consider one challenge new teachers often face within their first few years of teaching: after developing their knowledge through years of exposure and study, ideas become seemingly self-evident, rather than a process of figuring out relationships and patterns via conceptual leaps. In my own early years of teaching, I was constantly discovering that whatever I thought was the simplest way to explain something really wasn't. I would hear a student tell a peer to look at what I was describing in a different way, and then I'd recall moments from my own learning that had slipped from my memory as I pushed forward toward ever-newer complexities within my subject.

Technology works similarly, but with the added dynamic of incredibly rapid changes in the tools themselves. This rapidity can be intimidating, causing frustration for those of us who want to have mastered anything and everything that appears in our class. We may feel we can't keep up, we don't measure up, and we might as well give up on developing our technology skills.

However, I would contend there is another, more positive way to look at what the dizzying speed of change can mean for us: If you were to know everything there was to know about educational technology right now, in five minutes you'd be behind.

That's positive? Well, rather than this speed proving conclusive evidence that we should throw up our hands and not try, we can free ourselves of unrealistic expectations. Mastering it all is not—and cannot—be anyone's job, as no one is responsible for the impossible. Instead, we must find what can intrigue and inspire, and allow unfamiliar technology to become a meaningful part of learning—which, believe it or not, we can do without spending much on it.

Because at its core, seeing and acting on technology's potential for making a school great is a function of how our larger teams communicate about what to try and how to learn from the results.

Put another way, our goal is not simply to find good tools; rather, our goal is to find a way to communicate possibilities that make our school's personal and professional environment uplifting for all.

Chapter 3
Learning Successes

What kinds of successes make for a personally and professionally uplifting environment? Does your school identify, share, and build upon such successes?

Focusing on sustaining or building what makes a school genuinely distinctive requires a team of educators becoming comfortable discussing their school's strengths.

Among the strengths schools have been sharing and exploring for decades is a strong sports team. A team may have two, three, or more coaches, and the local newspaper may be in touch about results and upcoming challenges, so discussing possibilities for improvement comes naturally. That's due in large part to the fact that activities with an audience lead people to want to devote time and attention to them, because the team's successes (and its failures) are out in the open on public display.

I do believe having a strong athletics program can be a wonderful discussion point for any school wanting to convey its strengths, and athletics can certainly teach students invaluable skills, including teamwork, leadership, honorable winning, and graceful losing.

But regardless of how valuable sports and other extracurricular activities may be for the school and the community, we must remember that the fundamental purpose of school is academic; and for a school to be special, there should be noteworthy educational activities that all stakeholders recognize and share. Schools in which teachers and coaches work together to help their students succeed in all areas of their education are schools that have an important piece of the puzzle in place.

Let's return to our supermarket line scenario and the parents' question about what makes your school special. Know this: No informed parent with a choice would select a school without recognizable academic successes.

To truly paint a picture of your school as a special place, everyone who works there must strive to refine and improve learning activities constantly so they become more effective. Students attending a school that does this—a school where things are going well—tend to be confident in their ability to take on challenges.

These students know how to overcome barriers to success, and they know their school's staff can connect them with resources, programs, and people focused on their learning.

It may seem obvious that if a school's teachers don't meet regularly to discuss how to foster success and work with new ideas, the school will have far fewer successes to trumpet. It's like having a sports team that doesn't practice. Unfortunately, this kind of professional environment is all too common among American schools.

Starting to address this concern, however, is not difficult. It simply requires a point of departure for fostering stories of academic successes. We will begin with a framework that divides learning activities into four categories: the *powerfully memorable*, *the generally effective*, *the weak, but easy*, and *the waste of time*.

I should note that much of what follows focuses on classroom teachers' work, but in the very best schools, these teachers regularly draw upon both their teaching and non-teaching colleagues' insights to build the best kind of learning.

Let's take a look.

The Powerfully Memorable

No matter how well you deliver a lesson, it won't be effective unless your students are paying attention. Capturing their attention creates the environment your students need to grapple with an idea and connect it to other concepts and possibilities.

No matter how well you deliver a lesson, it won't be effective unless your students are paying attention.

But does capturing students' attention require entertaining them at a level they would get from digital media? Certainly, many teachers believe they are unable to compete with the television, the movies, the video games, and the music inundating our students.

However, while there is obvious appeal to the flash of these sources of entertainment, the truth is this: they can't compete with the power of a strong teacher.

Teachers connect on a personal level, and through this rapport, they create the conditions students need for believing in themselves. Strong teachers figure out what motivates a student, what personal challenges they need to navigate, and what to say to help the student avoid frustration and even despair. So while digital media may have its appeal, we are still a long way from digital media replicating what a strong teacher can do.

Capturing your students' attention is only the first step in creating powerfully memorable learning, though—and even then, doing so only creates the chance for great learning to happen.

Powerfully memorable learning possesses a variety of characteristics, but we'll start with several I have seen in exceptional learning activities. This is by no means an exhaustive list, but it is a good start.

Think back to kindergarten, elementary, middle, and high school, and recall your own great moments of learning. (This will be a longer stretch back in time for some of you, but whatever your age, the really amazing moments will stick out.) Which lessons, ideas, or activities have stuck in your head as moments when you saw the world in a new way?

I ask this question in the sessions and workshops I teach around the world, and I always love the responses. Here are several from recent talks:

- "We went out in a field and linked arms with younger students to replicate the size of the Titanic."

- "We had to use string and salt to pick up an ice cube."

- "In sixth grade, we played a game called 'Caravans,' and our groups needed to complete certain activities or develop skills to earn points for supplies."

- "We created a TV commercial."

- "We made abstract paintings for each chapter of a book and then presented our chapters to the class to explain their symbolism and connection."

- "We created a rainbow in the classroom."

- "We built pyramids with Home Depot orange buckets full of dirt, using simple tools."

Any of the scenarios in these responses could have allowed for new intellectual leaps, but the activity certainly didn't guarantee a moment of great learning. Rather, people remember the moments largely because of what their teachers made happen with them.

Keeping Learning Active

You'll notice one shared characteristic of these responses is that they are all active, hands-on experiences. We can contrast the interesting facets of the above with what some would call "sit-and-get."

Lectures are an easy target for those advocating for more active learning. For every master storyteller who consistently enthralls his or her students, there are probably a thousand or more instructors who simply talk at their classes, leaving them to wonder why their students don't recall what they covered. It isn't rocket science: there was broadcast, but little to no reception.

The follow-up complaint is loaded with failure: "I don't know what's wrong with these kids—I taught it to them!"

I believe that as responsible as we are for covering content, we are equally responsible for crafting how we deliver that content to maximize its reception. Take ownership of that responsibility, work with your colleagues to explore possibilities for ways to deliver your content creatively, and maybe even get your students' feedback about what works and what doesn't. Once you do these things, then you will be moving in the direction of the powerfully memorable.

Similarly, there are "activities" that are not only particularly un-active, but they accomplish little as well. Though most teachers have probably done a ream of them, I never hear someone say that worksheets generated really amazing learning.

Worksheets are a common way to do a certain amount of practice to fill a certain amount of time. Students who already understand the concepts find doing worksheets easy, and those who need more interactive learning find them miserable. And although worksheets are another easy target, I'll admit they can have some value, but it is only significant when the instructions prompt students to act on an idea, rather than merely identify a correct answer.

The real question is this: "What qualifies as 'truly memorable'?" What allows us to connect ideas that have previously seemed disparate or even impenetrable?

Achieving Excellence

Another shared characteristic I have heard in responses regarding memorable learning is that students find themselves achieving real excellence. They push themselves to achieve, and then a teacher who rarely tosses out a significant compliment will drop a "well done."

Infrequent praise isn't the point; it's the wording of the message that gives a clearer sense of what's important.

Many students look at assignments as hurdles that they simply work through to complete and get out of the way, so imagine turning in a project and hearing "well done." If you were to receive a "well done" because you had completed multiple revisions and adjustments to achieve something impressive, that's one thing. But in a setting focused on meaningful success, that's not a response you'd likely receive for a first draft. Instead, the teacher might say something along the lines of, "I like where this is going. Where do you intend to take it next?"

In today's society, we seem to praise children for very little. "Look at this drawing—you're a genius!" As any fan of educational researcher Carol Dweck knows, praising children for what they are, rather than what they've worked to accomplish, fosters a "fixed mindset," not a "growth mindset."

Students know when a teacher has something powerful to say, and they lose faith that praise has real meaning when it is frequent and effusive.

Breaking Predictability

Another characteristic of great learning is the interruption of the usual predictability of the classroom.

I have asked hundreds of audiences of teachers to tell me the one word that the average student would say when asked to describe school. The vast majority of the time, that word is "boring." Teachers of younger students may say something along the lines of "fun," "wonderful," or "fascinating." Heck, kindergartners may even show up and hug your leg, which, depending on how clean the child is, may be less charming than it sounds.

What fascinates me most about the wildly common response of "boring" is that the students don't mean it. They actually tend to like school—they like being around their friends, they appreciate a certain amount of structure (which they may not have much of at home), and they want to be around caring and stable adults (another element their homes may lack).

So why is "boring" such a common response? It's because the students have a limited vocabulary. It is true that some of their classes or learning time might prove rather tedious, but if the students had a greater vocabulary and a willingness to consider the question more in depth, they would probably say they find school "predictable."

Consider how your class starts each day. Is it five minutes of goals, followed by another five minutes of question-and-pair-share, and then something else, day-in and day-out? In my experience, when students think they know exactly will happen, they are less likely to be interested in what is going on.

This gets us back to the idea of capturing students' attention. A certain amount of predictability can make the classroom a safe place on a psychological level; however, for pulling some intrigue from the lesson, a lack of predictability can prove far more effective.

Discovering Knowledge

Another characteristic of powerfully memorable learning is giving students the chance to discover what they are supposed to learn, rather than simply tasking them with memorizing it.

Initially, it may seem to be more time-efficient to tell students exactly what they need to know and then expect them to handle it. For highly self-motivated students, that may suffice, but it leaves out the opportunity for fascinating interaction as students from a much broader swath of the class start making connections based on their own efforts.

As an example, please indulge me with a moment of Japanese grammar. Each year in the first semester of Japanese 1, I taught what is called the "-te" form of verbs. If a student misses this critical piece of how Japanese verbs work, a mountain of mistakes and accompanying confusion are on the horizon.

The traditional approach would have been to tell students in a stern tone how very important this lesson is and that they need to listen closely. It's possible that such an announcement would work, particularly if it's the first time they've heard it from me. Going forward, though, how much attention would students pay when I don't make this announcement? The challenge is how to get them to focus without compromising future possibilities; in essence, we want the moment to draw their attention all on its own.

So instead, I divided the students into groups and then put a set of verbs they had learned on one side of the screen, with the "-te" forms of the verbs on the other. I then asked the groups to look for and articulate a pattern for going from the first set to the second.

They talked with one another, and quite quickly identified the easier of the two rules they needed to know. One student—we'll call him Mark—raised his hand for the group and identified the rule (drop the "-ru" at the end of the verb and replace it with "-te"). I agreed that works for some of the verbs, and then had the groups identify which seemed to function that way. We then had the "Mark Rule" (the student for whom the rule was named would typically crack a big smile—it's cool to have your own rule).

We then jumped into the logic for the notably more interesting other main group of verbs; and after a while, we ended up with an "[insert the name of a precocious kiddo] Rule," and we were on our way with how to identify verb groupings, "-te" form construction, and the blessedly small handful of unusual verbs that worked differently.

All told, this normally took 30-40 minutes.

Would it have been quicker to hand them a sheet explaining the rules at the beginning? Sure. Would as many students have learned the concept as effectively? I don't think so. In my experience, the process of grappling with differences and developing a framework for thinking about a structure has proven more effective for helping students understand patterns than more mechanical approaches to teaching grammar.

Making It Meaningful

A final characteristic of powerfully memorable learning we'll consider in this section is that the activity is meaningful beyond the classroom. Another way to describe it is that the activity in some fashion transcends the grade.

All things being equal, when we task students with doing something they are interested in, they are more likely to devote substantial time to the project and less likely to finish it simply out of a desire to "be done." This observation is certainly not groundbreaking; and yet, so much of what students do every day offers nothing more compelling to them than the promise or threat of a grade.

Changing the audience for the students' work is one way to address this—when done well, that is.

In the 1990s, I would ask my students every so often to come up with skits using the vocabulary and grammar patterns we were studying.

"Alright, guys—on Friday, we'll take what we've been learning and do skits! It'll be fun!"

They would look back at me with facial expressions that said, "It'll be over soon."

Friday would roll around, and one group after another would come forward and produce something that fell squarely into the realm of The Lame. I chose not to identify it that way, figuring, "Well, that was lame!" wouldn't be a productive comment.

"Okay, good, and let's see what our next group has for us," I'd offer.

There would be that one student with a notable effort (he was typically trying to impress the girl on the other side of the room), but by and large what they inflicted on both their classmates and me simply and consistently wasn't good.

Then I convinced my principal that buying four iMacs (the turn-of-the-century ones with the colorful backsides) was a good idea. That fall, at the beginning of the term, I looked at my students who had taken Japanese with me the previous year, and I dropped this:

"Guys, this year, there will be no more skits." (Several students' eyebrows went up in a nice imitation of Spock, may he rest in peace.) "See those Macs in the back of the room? You'll be using them to create videos to show what you're learning." (Facial expressions showed they were intrigued.)

What a difference!

The first day we watched the students' projects, two things completely knocked me over:

First, the students were celebrating one another's work. After every video, they were clapping and tossing out "That was cool!" and "That was great!"

Mind you, I wasn't prompting them to do this—it was simply how they reacted. It made me wonder how many high-schoolers never hear anyone at home celebrating their academic accomplishments. Too many, I figure.

Second, the quality of their work had gone through the roof. Students who had barely been completing their homework were spending loads of time in my classroom after school, glued to the Macs, working to get their videos just right.

Where had all this talent been when they were doing their skits? The answer: buried in their fear of performing in front of their peers. This is the "done well" part of changing the audience. I'd given them a different stage with the skits, but had introduced a frightening component that neutralized the advantage of the larger audience.

Once I let students know everyone would make videos we would watch as a group, the dynamic changed considerably. Expanding their audience without forcing them to perform in front of the class had not only resulted in much more interesting projects, but also prompted a different attitude about the quality of their work, teaching me this:

When students know others will see their work, they want it to be good. When it's just for the teacher, they want it to be good enough.

I shared this observation with one of my audiences some years ago, and noticed that after the presentation many of the teachers had tweeted and retweeted it. I suspect many of the more profound observations about our work come not from carefully crafting a thought, but from merely sharing our insights. More to the point, talking with others about our work brings out the best in us.

However, my story aside, why don't our students put more effort into their day-to-day assignments? While there may be any number of solid answers, I think it comes down to how students see us as teachers.

The teacher, after all, is not simply the hopefully caring, stable adult running the show in the classroom. Rather, from our students' perspective, the teacher is also a forgiving person who will continue to encourage them, even when their work is well beneath what they are capable of producing.

How many of you have looked at a student and said, "I know you can do better work than this"?

How many? Somewhere between most and all, I'm guessing.

The students look back, confirm the teacher's statement as true, and perhaps promise to do better next time.

Done. On to the next project.

Having their peers in the classroom see their work is an entirely different matter. Doing a lame job in front of their friends and others may mean playful harassment for days, weeks, or longer. On the flip-side, creating something awesome earns a student all sorts of style points in the group's eyes.

"Meaningful" can reach another level again when done for an audience beyond the school's campus. For several years, my nonprofit, Next Vista for Learning, has done an annual contest challenging students to create videos telling their stories of service to others.[1] Typically, this means the student researches a nonprofit, learns its story, interviews volunteers, writes business letters asking for visuals they can incorporate into their project, gets feedback from their contacts, and so on.

---

[1] See winners of these contests here: http://www.nextvista.org/tag/projectwinner+serviceviavideo/

Finalists receive a $200 donation for an eligible charity or service effort, though the monetary donation often pales in comparison to the support and new volunteers a really strong video can attract. Students whose videos have earned finalist status often comment on what a powerful experience it is to learn that adults helping others in the community so gratefully received their work.

When students first learn that the possibilities of their work are not limited to what teachers ask them, and that what they do can make a difference in the larger community, they are having learning moments they will never forget.

All of these characteristics of learning activities—being active, exhibiting excellence, breaking predictability, requiring discovery, and pursuing the meaningful, along with many others—tend to show up in powerfully memorable learning. Still, a learning activity could show all of these characteristics and not be powerfully memorable for the student.

What makes a lesson memorable is how the activities with these characteristics interact and what inspires the student to go beyond what is simply required.

We'll look at a couple of examples for each of the categories of learning activities. For a project that meets the highest standard of powerfully memorable learning, we'll begin with Ann Makosinski's winning entry into the 2013 Google Science Fair.

Each year, Google holds a global science competition for teens, and in 2013, Ann of British Columbia, Canada, won the fifteen- to sixteen-year-old category. The video Google Science Fair released to tell Ann's story is a powerful discussion prompt, and if you want your school to reach its potential, it is well-worth the two minutes and seventeen seconds it takes to watch.[2]

At the time of the competition, Ann was a sixteen-year-old high school student. In the video's introduction, she tells us the students who enter science fairs aren't necessarily at the top of their classes; instead, they are simply people who question how things work. She describes her long-held interest in insects, marveling at how "they are so small, but so complicated."

The video then shifts to how she learned that a friend in the Philippines (where Ann's mother is from) had dropped out of school due to bad grades. It seems the

---

[2] Makosinski, Ann. "Can I power a flashlight without batteries?" YouTube video from Google Science Fair. 2:17. Posted February 11, 2014. https://www.youtube.com/watch?v=yrnNmzSSn0w

friend's family couldn't afford electricity, and without it, she had been unable to study at night.

Ann wondered if she could help people like her friend by creating a flashlight powered by the heat of the human hand. She then goes on to describe how she went about creating one using Peltier tiles. One of the many interesting things about Ann's story is that her excitement didn't come just from seeing her creation become a concrete success, but that it inspired within her a hope that she might help the hundreds of millions of people worldwide without electricity.

When I share Ann's story in sessions at summits and conferences, I always ask the audience what strikes them most. People mention she is curious without thinking of herself as some "genius nerd," the personal reasons she began exploring the issue of light for those without electricity, the access to resources and equipment that allowed her to experiment, the encouragement by those around her, and so on.

After we discuss these thoughts, I ask the group, "If Ann were a student at your school, would you celebrate her accomplishments?" The response is always a resounding, "Yes."

I then ask, "How do you know she isn't at your school?"

And while we all know from the video where Ann is from, the point is never lost on the group: There may be students just like her on their campuses. These are students who are *so close* to creating something amazing, but they may not have had the encouragement to make the leap to giving it a try.

Powerfully memorable learning makes you leave behind the day-to-day checking off of boxes that passes for assessment. While, yes, a certain amount of keeping things organized and moving forward is necessary for traditionally constructed school settings, I suspect we don't ask ourselves often enough whether what we are doing is something that our students will recall in a year, in a decade, or throughout their lifetimes.

Like us, our students remember the moments when we allow them to surprise themselves by discovering capabilities they didn't know they had. They remember the moments when they realize their hard work allowed them to go beyond what was required and achieve excellence that would have been otherwise unattainable. They remember the moments of creative exploration resulting in meaningful discoveries that help other people, especially those in need.

These are the moments that become stories for friends and family for years to come. In other words, powerfully memorable learning shows us we have something new to give, and it is likely a realization that we are capable of something new—or much more than we ever thought.

Another way to look at powerfully memorable learning is to consider what it isn't.

Anything designed merely to check off a box in a gradebook is not likely powerfully memorable learning.

Anything for which it is hard to explain why you're doing it is not likely powerfully memorable learning.

And anything that requires students to do nothing more than sit and listen is not likely powerfully memorable learning.

Anything that requires students to do nothing more than sit and listen is not likely powerfully memorable learning.

Ann's effort in the Google Science Fair may seem to be something remarkably few would ever accomplish. Looking at the above descriptions, though, it is hopefully clear that every student can have the kinds of moments we are exploring.

During the 2006-2007 school year, I taught a video production class to a group of seventh and eighth graders at a school in Santa Clara, California. It was my first time with middle schoolers, and I found them to be the neediest group of human beings I'd ever encountered. That said, I rather liked them anyway, and they probably taught me more about good teaching than any other class I have had.

About midway through the first semester, I charged my quirky kiddos with creating a video that teaches something. All of us have had the experience of sitting in a class and thinking, "I have no idea what this teacher is telling me." Most of us have also had someone say, "Hey, look at it this way," and that helped us get past our confusion. My goal was for them to generate such a moment with a short video.

They went to work, but one student got up and walked my way. We'll call him Joe.

"Hey, Mr. Hurley," said Joe with a tone that implied confidence was MIA that day.

"Yeah, Joe, what you got?"

"I, um, I can't do this project," he offered.

"What do you mean? You've made videos before," I countered.

"It's not the video; it's the teaching thing." A short pause ensued. "I suck at school," he said, defeated.

"Well, first, you don't need to use that verb. And 'at school'? You're breaking my heart! I could almost understand if it were one subject, but at everything? That's not right."

"I'm just not good at this stuff."

"Come on, I'll bet you know something you could teach. How about a math trick?"

"No, I suck at math."

"Well, there's that verb again. Are you telling me you don't know one math trick?"

"Well, I know one…"

"Alright! Let's make a video."

Joe went on to create a video about learning to multiply by nines. You can see it at nextvista.org/multiply-by-nines/; it's pretty short, so don't blink.

We posted this video in the NextVista.org library, and at any point later in the year, I was positively armed and ready for Joe. Picture the subsequent conversation:

Joe, with some new assignment: "Mr. Hurley, I can't do this!"

"Time out. That's what you said when we did the video to teach something. Do you remember? You made that one about multiplying by nine. We put it on my nonprofit's website, and there may be hundreds or thousands of kids around the world learning their nines because of you."

And how does he respond? And I quote: "Oh yeah, huh?"

You gotta love 'em.

Something shared with the world, something that can help others, something that represented more than what a student might think he or she is capable of doing—all of this is the kind of powerfully memorable learning that happens in classrooms around the world every day.

We will explore lesser levels of learning next, but at its core, pursuing powerfully memorable learning (and teaching) is no simple matter. However you approach it, one of the key components is regularly sharing stories of both what has and hasn't worked in your efforts to unlock the spectacular.

While powerfully memorable learning is certainly the ideal, it is not the only kind of beneficial teaching and learning. Let's explore the second category in this acronym-less framework more deeply.

The Generally Effective

If the powerfully memorable is the most potent type of learning activity we can construct for our students, and if we assume that most, and perhaps all, teachers cannot create this kind of learning day-in and day-out, then there must be another level that works well. It may not produce what students will recall decades later, but it is what we will call "generally effective" learning.

At this level of learning, teachers capture their students' attention and guide them as they explore content in productive ways. In so doing, they optimize the chances for moments of powerfully memorable learning going forward. These moments may not wield the life-changing punch of our first category, but they are still valuable.

When I was a junior in high school, I had a fascinating chemistry teacher by the name of Mr. Plyler. One day, he started class by holding up an egg.

"You'll be in pairs, and each pair will have an egg," he said. "You'll have some cardboard, masking tape, and some other materials. Your job is to create a container that will keep the egg from breaking when I throw it off the building."

My buddy Paul and I *waaaay* overthought this, including using water balloons as shock absorbers. I say this because at the one moment it mattered (to the egg, in particular), we ended up setting free the previously confined yolk from its prison. That's how I'll characterize the result of our effort.

Without going into further detail about our egg's demise, I will say that the egg drop is one of only a handful of class activities I recall from middle school and high school in any significant detail.

It's not that my teachers were bad at what they did, or even that the classes themselves were gratingly tedious—it's just that very little left the bounds of the expected, and as someone who could navigate quite easily what was asked of me academically, I admit I was on autopilot plenty of the time.

I would place the cool egg activity in the realm of the "generally effective," not because it isn't memorable (obviously, it is for me), but because I don't recall how it connected to what we were studying or how it affected my subsequent learning. This is a good time to note that a learning activity's category will differ from student to student. (I must add that Mr. Plyler created many powerfully memorable moments of learning, and I will come back to his wonderful talents later.)

In a world of rampant grade inflation (or at least in the United States), not achieving the top tier of any given scale may feel personally deflating, but remember: teachers whose work is normally generally effective are teachers whom you want to have on your school's staff.

That's because students in a generally effective teacher's classroom tend to learn what they need to, they can draw connections to other areas of study, they can confidently express their handling of the content, and they experience many of the characteristics of great learning. While these activities may or may not contain significant public relations value for the school, they're still good for learning.

Technology can greatly help in creating conditions for generally effective learning.

Imagine you are a middle school or high school student entering a classroom. As you begin to settle into your chair, your teacher starts class by explaining the logistics of the day's lesson. The degree to which you pay attention to your teacher and the lesson will depend on whether you are hungry, the degree to which other (typically personal) things are on your mind, and how many potentially distracting elements are within your field of vision. And if this is how most of the teacher's classes begin, then, as we discussed earlier, your familiarity with the predictable process can make it difficult to ratchet up your attention to the level that you need to work constructively with the day's lesson.

If the purpose of our educational system is to merely identify those students with the self-discipline to focus under adverse circumstances, we're doing great. If you are like me, though, you probably prefer a system that seeks to foster success by bringing out students' creativity and potential to innovate and by generating fascination with the topic's intricacies.

Now, imagine this: As class begins and you settle into your chair, the teacher says, "I have a picture I want you to see." She then moves to her computer to call up an image for the group to consider.

I would argue that at that moment, chances are pretty high that students are paying notably more attention to their teacher than they were during the more predictable launch of the class described earlier. Why?

Because the element of the unknown is intriguing.

Put yourself in the student's position. The image about to appear before you may be something you know or something you've never seen. It may be of a place nearby, far away, or off the planet. There may be people you know; you might even be in the picture. The image may be something in the now, a record of something in the past, or a vision of the future. What you are about to see may not even conform to the rules of physics.

All of that unknown—that lack of the predictable—is interesting.

All of that unknown—that lack of the predictable—is interesting.

Now imagine you're the teacher and consider an image's ability to create connections for your students. Perhaps you are teaching a lesson on energy and the environment, and you use figures 1 and 2 (on the following page) in your presentation.

Students looking at these images may come up with any number of questions to explore ways of powering a train, but the connections certainly don't stop there.

A student may have had a lifelong love of model trains, and this could be the most exciting moment of the year for him. Another may have an interest in the connections between locomotives, cowboys, and America's westward expansion. Another student's family may have emigrated from Japan, and this visual reminder in the second image of her heritage may be personally powerful.

Figure 1: Train
Credit: formatc1 from Flickr (CC by-sa 2.0),
https://www.flickr.com/photos/formatc1/2455108405/

Figure 2: Shinkasen
Credit: freddie boy from Flickr (CC by-sa 2.0),
https://www.flickr.com/photos/froderik/6921375430/

The point is, teachers who create compelling connections (positive ones, of course) for students tend to be the teachers whom students trust to be interesting. That trust makes for better classes. Better classes make for fewer discipline problems. Interested and engaged students make for an atmosphere everyone prefers. Rocket science, this is not.

Underlying this example is finding an interesting image or two. This is not a complicated use of technology, but the simple act of projecting an image only sets the stage—it is how we use the moment that makes for effective learning.

Consider Figure 3 (on the following page), a photo I took during a trip to Indonesia.

If you were to show Figure 3 to your class, you might make the mistake of asking something along the lines of, "What is this?" Though that may seem like an innocuous question, it falls into the "Do you know the right answer?" category of questions, which works against creating good conditions for learning.

The idea that asking for the right answer is counter-productive to learning may surprise many teachers, but consider what happens when we ask such a question. More often than not, asking this type of question

Figure 3: Borobudur at Ground Level
Credit: Rushton Hurley (CC by 4.0),
https://www.instagram.com/p/Bl1OHUGgJw2/

leads the bulk of the class to clam up and defer to the three or four students who always seem to know the right answer.

Our job as educators is not to validate the living daylights out of a handful of students while the rest of the class looks on; rather, it is to engage every single student at a frequency that allows them to develop intellectual confidence in their ability to discuss what they encounter.

So how could you approach a "Do you know the right answer?" moment more effectively? One simple way is to ask a question that prompts discussion without making a student feel their answer will be either right or wrong.

For example: "Okay, class, take a look at this picture, and in your groups, come up with at least three stories as to what this could be. Feel free to craft ones that seem a bit crazy—I want to see what kind of connections you can draw." This kind of prompt changes the classroom dynamic considerably. Now students will begin to interact with much less fear of instant judgment.

In addition to releasing the shackles associated with a correct answer, there's a very good reason to direct students to come up with at least three stories: Any given image may elicit a common answer as to what it is, but after one or two easy interpretations, students will probably find themselves having to reach a bit to get to their third answer. That is to say, the conditions are ripe for creative exploration of the topic.

It's worth noting that researchers like Gerard Puccio of the University at Buffalo (whose work inspired this example), have shown that creativity is not something you either have or you don't have. Instead, like anything else requiring practice, regularly tasking students with initiating creative responses not only gives them a sense that they can be creative, but in a group setting, it also develops opportunities to craft an environment that welcomes cool, interesting ideas.

As educators, we have an added motive for getting our students comfortable with their creativity: bluntly put, when they are creative, our teaching becomes more fun and more interesting. If you have ever graded a set of essays or slide presentations that all look and sound about the same, then you understand the desire to find something sharp to thrust into your skull while reading or watching the same lame thing over and over again.

Several years ago, I was working with teachers in a professional development program, and after dividing them into groups, I asked each group to come up with a set of geographic facts. One person created a shared slide presentation for his or her group and then gave each person a slide. Each member then thought of a geographic fact and placed it at the top of the slide.

One teacher wrote, "Grapes grow in Italy."

All good. It's true, and it's a nice point of departure for my next task, which was for the group members to go to their group's slides and, on each one, add a question that stemmed from the fact. The follow-up questions appearing on the slide with our grapes statement were:

- "What else grows in Italy?"
- "What products come from grapes?"
- "Where else are grapes grown?"

After giving the groups enough time to come up with the questions, I asked if they had added questions to each slide in the group. They had. I then asked, "Are the questions you wrote fascinating?"

The groups responded with stares, followed by someone saying, "Give us another couple of minutes."

I did.

After a few minutes of work, their questions had taken quite the leap. The teacher with the "Grapes grow in Italy" fact now had these questions on her slide:

- "How is climate change affecting Italy's grapes, and how does this compare/contrast with other grape-growing regions?"

- "How do winemakers create consistency in wine production?"

- "Have Italy's sales of wine been affected by the ever-growing popularity of Napa and Sonoma County winemakers?"

Note that the second set of questions came from the same people, in the same place, doing the same activity, at almost the same time. The one difference was the request to make their work "fascinating."

While wine production may not be the perfect topic for children, the bottom line is that asking your classes to make their work fascinating isn't hard, and it may very well result in something far more interesting for both you and your students.

Will the students do fascinating work? Some will, and some won't. But when you're grading piles of work on a given topic, having some fascinating submissions can carry you through without your frustration producing any self-inflicted harm.

The student project—which students typically present to their class, academic team, or even a larger group (think back to the relationship between audience and quality of work)—is another example of effective learning. When done well, projects give students the chance to build their confidence in mastering something researched as well as the opportunity to develop their communication skills, especially when addressing unfamiliar topics.

The term "project" can describe an endless array of learning activities, so for our purposes, we'll focus on the one aspect that I find most important: students exploring a topic in more detail than would be possible with the entire class. Ideally, the project also allows students to explore their interests alongside your course's content in a way that strengthens both their engagement and effort.

The shape your students' projects take in your classroom will largely depend upon the tools and resources you make available, how much flexibility you and your students have over learning time, and your comfort with allowing students to explore content beyond your subjects of expertise. Assuming the outcome is a presentation (either in person or in a crafted or recorded format), helping your students push themselves as they work toward their presentation and then preparing them to create successful presentations will be the keys to making the projects academically effective.

Kevin Brookhouser's book, *The 20Time Project*, is an exceptional exploration of how a student project can become something not merely effective, but powerfully memorable.

By studying the creativity-generating practices of companies like Google and 3M (going as far back as the 1950s), Brookhouser helped students create "20 percent time projects." In these projects, students spend a portion of their time in deep exploration of topics they find fascinating, and are pushed to take their exploration to new levels of academic excellence with mentors and action plans showing how what they learned inspired them to act. If you want to guide your students' efforts to new heights, *The 20Time Project* is a compelling read.

For our purposes, the presentations themselves become vehicles of possibility, whether of the scale Brookhouser describes or something less involved.

That's because for the student, the presentation in any form can become evidence of what they can do when they push themselves to create something excellent.

For teachers, these presentations become conversation starters with colleagues on how to tease the best work out of students and how to approach course content in ways that engage those who hadn't previously connected with the material.

For school and district leaders, short, recorded presentations become concrete examples of the learning taking place in their schools. This can be PR gold, and students' work can guide discussions about the kind of support school leaders should seek from the community based on intersections between students' work and the strengths of local (or not-so-local) companies and organizations.

Consider some of the projects Brookhouser's students chose and developed in the 2014–2015 school year:

- Collecting plastic bags and then crocheting them into sleeping mats for the homeless
- Organizing and teaching poetry workshops at a local elementary school
- Volunteering at a care home that tends to developmentally disabled clients

- "Busting myths" about the flu shot by creating a PSA and sharing it with local schools and hospitals

- Designing a web page so that hospital patients could more easily order food

You can watch a video with Brookhouser's students summarizing their projects in this short YouTube video.[3] You might even choose to watch it with colleagues in your department or grade level. I guarantee it will spark discussion.

Projects like the ones Brookhouser's students created easily make their way into the realm of generally effective, and most enter the top tier of powerfully memorable. One of the most important components of the generally effective it that at its core, such learning creates the conditions for students to take their work to the highest level.

The Weak, but Easy

It seems the busier we are, the more likely we are to handle challenges in ways that may not be all that effective, but will solve an issue of the moment. For us, the issue may be that we need to teach something, but that

---

[3] https://www.youtube.com/watch?v=3_TOarCXYrw

is entirely different from the issue of students needing to learn.

In other words, out of a need to generate some kind of a plan, it becomes easier to come up with something passive for our students than to craft a more active, more effective, and more memorable learning experience.

Enter the "sit and listen while I lecture" plan.

I'll preface by noting that, by definition, lectures are not a weak teaching tool. Some teachers can paint vivid pictures for their listeners, bringing a number of possibilities forward before revealing the idea that beautifully ties everything together. These master storytellers use language to intrigue and inspire, and their lectures are a treat to experience.

Unfortunately, I think it is safe to say that the vast majority of the teachers who lecture don't fall into this category. Instead, they talk without ever providing their students with much to think about, merely expecting them to recall what they said later on. These teachers offer few, if any, pointers to fascinating connections, never allowing their students to build confidence in drawing together content within and across disciplines.

Having students parrot back what we teach, though, does allow us to check off the "yes, I taught that" box. I should point out that "teach" in this statement means that the idea of "teaching" has been stretched to include merely mentioning something in the presence of those tasked with learning it.

Writer Arthur C. Clarke said, "Teachers that can be replaced by a machine should be." Clearly, as teachers our job is not merely putting something in front of our students; rather, we are (or should be) required to guide them in learning and extending upon ideas in a meaningful way. As we noted before, another way of saying this is that we, as teachers, are responsible for both the broadcast and reception of our content.

> We, as teachers, are responsible for both the broadcast and reception of our content.

It is true that some students, for any number of reasons, are barely able to pay attention, and not all of our students will do well with what we teach. Being great at what we do, however, means that despite this reality, we give up on no one because we never know what might move a child from seemingly hopeless to alive with excitement for possibilities. So we keep trying. For some of our students, the fact that we keep trying at all may be the seed that ultimately allows them to escape the personal and emotional barriers keeping them from succeeding.

Lectures are not the only weak-but-easy types of learning activities; another is the student project.

"Wait," you say. "Wasn't that an example of the 'generally effective'?"

Yes, but the quality of a project's learning experience depends upon what the student has to do for the project. If the sum total of the project is simply finding a few charts and paragraphs online, printing them out, and then attaching them to a cardboard tri-fold, that likely doesn't come all that close to "effective."

It is certainly possible that students will learn something from having found the items that grace the cardboard; however, without showing a command of the material, meaningfully connecting it to other content, and even providing insights that follow from the connections, we're stuck in some seriously lower-order thinking.

We can move such an assignment from intellectually barren to genuinely interesting, though, in a number of ways.

Imagine adding a follow-up assignment to the printouts and tri-fold board activity and having students follow citing the facts and paragraphs they find by evaluating their sources.

Imagine having students present their topic with a meaningful comparison to and contrast with another topic from a different course, such as linking Africa's nineteenth-century European colonization to what fish do when food is dropped into their tanks. Is that a good comparison? Why or why not? Defend your answer!

Or imagine that in the follow-up activity students present their content in a way that suggests something is not as it appears, followed by an exploration of how and why someone might do such a thing. Do people try to deceive us in the modern world? How do you know? How can you prove it? Why might someone choose a deceptive path? Should a society protect those targeted for this deception? If so, how?

Any of these ideas for follow-up activities would easily move the student project into the realm of the generally effective, and perhaps higher, giving students enough creative room to continue building upon their effort.

Weak teaching happens for all sorts of reasons, but I suspect one of the key causes is a sense that we don't have time to be creative.

Warning: I'm about to step on toes.

Yes, society at large asks teachers to fill a phenomenal number of roles. We aren't paid accordingly, but we do get the occasional person telling us that what we do is "noble." That probably doesn't make sense as a trade-off, but I would say that in terms of the meaning and sense of fulfillment that our work provides us, we are in a good position—those teachers who make their work meaningful, that is.

I have heard many, many teachers utter the following sentence (or some variation of it), and I believe I have even said it myself at some point in my twenty-five-plus-year career: "You want me to do what? I barely have enough time to get through the curriculum as it is!"

What I needed at that moment was a caring colleague to look me in the eye and reply, "You barely have enough time, *given the way you teach*."

(If you were reading quickly—and just in case you didn't catch it—*that* was the stepping-on-toes part.)

Understand, this is not meant as a digit-trodding denunciation—it's a message of hope.

The message is that there are different ways to teach effectively, and we can test those methods with students so that they (and we) find much more satisfaction in what we do together. One of the more exciting components of this contention is that the different method we pursue may be something that saves us time and allows us to reach students who haven't succeeded with what we have done to date.

At core, the message is this: Every last one of us can improve, and the most trying parts of our teaching won't be hanging around our necks forever.

We'll explore this idea in more detail in "Chapter 5: Individual Confidence." For the moment, though, let's move into our last category of learning activities.

The Waste of Time

As devoid of the fascinating that's typical of activities falling into the "Weak, but Easy" category, there is another category even further down the scale toward academic oblivion that I call "Waste of Time."

There is probably no greater stress on educators than time. Those in school offices need time to ensure processes and information are in place. Those in classrooms need time to cover swaths of curricula, all the while navigating our students' endless array of social and emotional needs. Those managing a school need time to focus on our campus community's creative possibilities, rather than the daily fires that threaten to consume our passion for helping teachers make great things happen.

And yet...

There are moments when teachers make decisions about how to use their limited time, out of fatigue or otherwise, that are incredibly difficult to justify from a professional perspective.

Imagine a teacher saying, "Everybody has been so good this week, I think on Friday we'll watch a movie!"

While the mountain of problems packed into that one statement might leave many of us to wonder where to begin offering our criticisms, I'd like to start by saying that it's better not to suggest to our students that by being comfortably compliant, we can take a day off and avoid that annoying learning thing.

Upon hearing the suggestion that the teacher thinks the class should take a day off, it might prove rather challenging for the students to pinpoint why they see their teacher as a professional who helps them make intellectual strides and develop a wonder for the unknown.

In fact, the teacher would likely be hard-pressed to explain how a movie, even if it does overlap with the topics their class is covering, is a productive way of preparing students for the assessments that follow.

At this point, the teacher who uttered such a line might stop me and lean over long enough to quietly note, "What I really need is more time to get some grading done."

An encouraging colleague might suggest that perhaps the teacher needs to reevaluate how many assignments they give their students or how they go about giving assessments.

While there are certainly those whose feedback to the students normally involves oodles of time (those who teach writing come to mind), for too many of us, time management is an area where new ideas may prove helpful.

We have to ask ourselves: how much learning takes place when we use our time to do something? If showing a movie were to enhance learning substantially, then showing a movie would be preferable to a less effective alternative.

And if while showing the movie, the teacher were to regularly stop it and discuss the story's development, examine the validity of the points it is making, or creatively brainstorm connections to the class's current content, that's one thing. On the other hand, giving students a "free period" is something entirely different.

About twenty years ago in a staff meeting, my school's principal looked at everyone and started the meeting by saying, "I understand that some of you are giving kids 'free periods.' Let me know if you plan to continue this, and if so I can arrange for you to work for free."

You've gotta love a great line.

Even activities that may seem like an integral part of our classes can fall into the "Waste of Time" category. Case in point: the fifty-problem practice set, a common assignment found in many math classes. (I randomly chose the number fifty, but replacing it with an "X" might be more appropriate.)

As a world languages teacher, I certainly understand the importance of practice. That said, we still have to defend what we ask students to do.

Back to the set of fifty practice problems, do we have all the needed variations of working with the problem represented? If those, let's say, four or five variations are represented correctly and distributed evenly, do we really need students to do ten or twelve of each? Would two or three suffice?

If two or three would work, is the reason for the larger number due to a lack of thought, a desire to keep our students busy, or something else?

As students work on these problems, are we moving throughout our classroom to help those struggling to overcome gaps with prior concepts, or do we tell them to be quiet, offering little to no help as they flounder?

What if we were to make not only the problem set much smaller, but also have students explain at least two common mistakes their peers make when incorrectly working on solving the problems?

What if you had pairs or groups come up with creative approaches to conveying how to avoid pitfalls when solving the problems, and then had them put those approaches into videos that eventually become part of a larger resource they post online and share with students elsewhere?

What if we challenged our students to come up with new ways of solving the problems, giving bonus points, style points, or kudos to those who add to their solutions one or more questions that we can't answer? That is to say, what if we taught our students how to anticipate upcoming topics by identifying the limits of what we are covering at the moment? Taking opportunities to have students use what they've learned to guess at what they'll study next is a great way to prepare the ground for the next unit.

Let's consider one more example of a learning activity that could be characterized as a waste of time: student projects. Yes, we've used student projects as an example in two other categories of learning activities. In this case, however, imagine a student going home, telling a parent about the project, and then the parent actually doing the work of putting the project together for the student.

The student does nearly (or exactly) nothing beyond announcing the project to their parent, and the teacher may end up in a parent meeting that is more about the parent's work than what the student needs to succeed.

Perhaps that is preferable to a financial audit. Perhaps.

Categorizing Learning

In this chapter, we've talked about the four categories of learning activities: the powerfully memorable; the generally effective; the weak, but easy; and the waste of time.

However, labeling these learning moments is not nearly as important as the reflection and action that follow them. What did you ask your students to do? Were the students able to do it? Will your students still be able to do what you asked in a week, a month, or a year? Can your students take what they learned to another level, connecting it to other topics and experiences, identifying and exploring unanswered questions, and creatively articulating ways others might encounter it?

Remember, none of us is a perfect educator, and even the best lesson we ever teach can be improved upon or expanded in some way. As we look at what we craft for our students, at our best, we should see stories that will live in their hearts and minds and essentially convey what our school can be for the community.

We turn next to these stories, as well as to the personal and professional experiences and interactions that foster them.

Chapter 4

Exploratory Culture

How would you describe the professional culture at your school?

Do your colleagues regularly share ideas? Do they debate approaches to improving programs and curricula? Do school leaders and teachers collaborate to share stories of successes regularly? Do you have fun exploring ideas together? Are people comfortable disagreeing with one another?

Barriers to and opportunities for strengthening the professional team exist at every school, and in this chapter, we'll explore a variety of possibilities, starting with a school that—among the schools I have worked at or visited—sets the bar for professional communication.

Serra's Strength

I have visited northern California's Junipero Serra High School more than a hundred times over the last seven years. Rather than hiring a full-time staff member dedicated to instructional technology, they bring me in. The flexibility works well both for me and for the school, and each year, I remind them that when they are ready to hire someone else, I'll gladly do as much as I can to help make the transition easy and productive.

While I wouldn't describe Serra (or any other school) as perfect, it does have one particular strength that every school should strive to cultivate: The adults working there are comfortable disagreeing with one another and exploring how their perspectives differ.

When telling other educators about this strength, I often use this short exchange as an example:

> Teacher 1: "I think we need to look
>   more at [insert topic]."
>
> Teacher 2: "I don't, but talk to me."

For the vast majority of Serra's staff, neither the first teacher's contention nor the second's reply creates an interpersonal problem—these are professionals genuinely interested in how their colleagues think, and they are comfortable agreeing to disagree. The school's leadership considers the input of its teachers when making decisions, but the staff understands that they will not always get what they want. Non-teaching members of the team also contribute to discussions about the school's direction.

Junipero Serra High School is a place where, quite simply, people listen to one another.

This is an important strength, but rather than holding up the school's professional interaction as a desired result, I consider it a powerful means to something better, a critical component for creating an exploratory culture, and, ultimately, a truly special school.

Schools with an exploratory culture are filled with people (everyone who works and learns there) who are comfortable communicating with one another about possibilities, both simple and challenging.

The ideas showing promise do not remain trapped in the discussion; instead, they become memorable learning experiences—as activities, projects, and programs— that everyone knows they can contribute to and make even better.

Take, for example, when Serra adopted a block schedule. The school's leadership suggested replacing a period schedule that had been in place for almost forty years, so overcoming inertia would obviously prove a challenge.

Teachers and school leaders looked together at a variety of models, including visits to schools where the models were already in place. The leadership finally suggested Serra try one schedule as a two-week pilot project in the spring of 2012 to see what teachers thought of it. If successful, it would go into effect that fall.

The teachers hated it.

As a result, the leadership canceled plans for the change and went back to the drawing board, working with a team of teachers to craft a second pilot to try in the spring of 2013.

The results of the second pilot? The teachers decided they could try it, so the leadership promised to survey them at the end of each semester during the 2013–2014 school year and revert to the old schedule if the teachers voted to do so. That school year, the surveys overwhelmingly showed teachers were either positive or very positive about the change, and the schedule has been in place at Serra since.

I once asked the principal about the effort to adopt a block schedule, particularly the effort with the first pilot.

"Well," he said, "one thing to know about asking people's opinions is that you might not hear what you want."

The fact that he and the rest of the leadership acted upon what the teachers conveyed after the first pilot did not merely show the school's strength in how it operated as a team—it resulted in a model that has proved beneficial for almost everyone.

In that same vein, I have been to schools where what is best for the school loses out to the needs of a few individual egos. It does not require an advanced degree to understand that this generates bitterness and seriously lessens the chance for the initiative's success.

When teams are truly willing to explore possibilities, however, there is a confidence that what is decided together will ultimately be best for both the students and the adults.

Perhaps the best expression of an exploratory culture, however, is when a school puts forth an organized, concerted effort to share success stories made possible by its community members. As we'll see, sharing stories about what seems promising, or has proved effective or even exceptional, allows a school to accelerate the fostering of successes. These successes then help answer our original question, "What makes your school special?"

Discussing Successes

If you could create your "ideal school," how would you describe it? Can you picture the buildings and facilities? How many students would be on campus and in each class? What learning opportunities would your school offer? How would the students be known within the greater community?

If you could create your "ideal school," how would you describe it?

You could look at your ideal school from any number of angles, but for the school you imagine, let's focus on these questions: What would your role be as a member of your ideal school's team? More to the point, how would you and your colleagues interact?

Too often, we imagine our ideal school from the standpoint of what resources the school would have, what activities our students would engage in, and the level of freedom teachers would have to teach. Less often in this imaginative exercise do we paint a picture of our ideal school in terms of collegiality. Granted, you would want to be in a school with people you like and respect, but that is different than knowing *how* you would work together.

Perhaps in your ideal school, teachers would teach fewer hours. With some of the remaining time, everyone would take on duties commonly handled by administrative staff or campus leaders. Adding this element of adult interaction could allow for more philosophical discussions, promote creative brainstorming, and balance the rather different experience of "being on stage" as a teacher.

When I was an assistant language teacher in the junior high and high schools of Japan's Goto Islands in Nagasaki Prefecture, I witnessed this kind of arrangement firsthand. There, teachers in secondary schools typically taught three classes a day and with some of the time they didn't teach, they took care of tasks that would typically be handled by assistant principals or others in the United States.

While I admire much of what the Japanese do, I know there is plenty for which I will never fully understand the value. Yet I was impressed by how frequently everyone working at all levels interacted. In my time as a teacher and a principal in the United States, I've seen few schools where teachers engage with one another as constructively, professionally, and intellectually as those I met while working in Japan.

Among the schools I have seen and where I have worked around the world, the best are ones where adults, especially teachers, feel comfortable sharing ideas, easily discussing things that don't go well, and creating resources to pass along to colleagues on and off their campuses.

Communication Barriers

If I were dreaming up my ideal school, the ability to comfortably share ideas and resources would be a primary component. It may sound strange to those professionally outside of education, but one of the biggest problems schools have is a reluctance to share stories of success effectively.

This reluctance may be based on the belief that openly discussing one teacher's successes represents a critique of other teachers' shortcomings. In this kind of setting, a leader who refers to a teacher's good work might be inadvertently creating the conditions for that teacher to becoming ostracized. This sort of dysfunctional atmosphere is distressingly common.

When considering how to overcome this poisonous lack of professional interaction, a good point of departure is understanding the substantial advantages of doing so, including the following.

First, teachers can let go of the absurdity that we never do anything wrong. The simple realization that every single one of us has room for improvement can allow for discussions that promote interesting and needed growth.

Second, students benefit from an environment in which we regularly ask one another for, and act on, ideas for varying our presentation and exploration of content to reach more of our classes.

Third, when we don't come across as know-it-alls, conversations with parents and other stakeholders allow for new possibilities. Parents appreciate when we collaboratively discuss possibilities for fostering their children's new talents. You'll also find that community supporters may be more prepared to give their time and resources when we are open about how we are working to overcome the barriers we and our students face.

Fourth, and perhaps most important, students tend to have a stronger rapport with teachers who talk *with* them rather than *at* them, and this better rapport can lead to more effective learning conditions.

This includes getting students' feedback on how a class is going and how we can be better teachers for them, something I would do from time to time. When I'd have this conversation with my students, I would remind them that while I couldn't promise I would act on their suggestions, if they were willing to share their ideas (even the critical ones), I did feel I could improve.

Once, when I asked a class this, a girl in the far corner of the class raised her hand. She was probably as far from me as one could be in the room. I called on her, and as she began to speak, she looked at her desk.

"Mr. Hurley, you always call on the same people."

Ouch. That was difficult to hear, especially in front of the group. I don't even think I knew I'd gone down that problematic path.

"Wow. That's an important thing for me to know. I promise I'll do better."

And I did. Why? Because in front of everyone I said I would. That moment was an opportunity not merely to show that I could keep from committing an easily identified teacher foul—it was also a golden chance to let my students know I listen to them.

We all fall into habits that work against our hopes for what we want to accomplish and how we want our students to respond. But maintaining open communication with our students and colleagues is a prerequisite for most, and perhaps all, substantive kinds of organizational improvement.

When we begin approaching how to build a better atmosphere to discuss possibilities for better teaching and learning, one of the first challenges we face is creating concrete avenues for identifying strengths. All too often, these strengths are hidden behind a silence—one brought on by an atmosphere that discourages discussing successes and can deprive both our students and teachers of moments they would treasure. With a clear sense of how to discuss and explore successes, however, a team can orient itself toward innovating in exciting ways.

Knowing Your School

It was the early 1990s and I was in my second year of teaching. I was working at a large, overcrowded, comprehensive public high school on the east side of San Jose, California. Like many fairly new teachers, I had volunteered for all sorts of activities, in part because I had a boundless idealism about who we were and could be as a high school. As I saw it, high school is where students discover and pursue possibilities, where they begin to experience intellectual joy, and where they become citizens who honor and improve our communities.

Over time, my optimism has become more measured. While I still believe high school is a place and time where students discover their potential, I have also learned to devote my time to efforts that allow me to keep a more balanced load on my shoulders.

At that time, my volunteerism included serving on several committees. (This was before I had figured out that, for most teachers, being on a committee is to teaching as a root canal is to dental hygiene.)

One day I walked over to my friend Brian's classroom to pick up some paperwork as part of gathering evidence of our school's efforts ahead of an accreditation visit. Brian was a world history teacher, meaning he had been optimistically charged with covering a good portion of everything that has ever happened.

He was also a "tables teacher."

Unlike many "desks teachers," who regularly focus on how to minimize the chances of losing control of their classes by distributing students most likely to annoy one another or the teacher (or both) among the rows of desks, tables teachers focus on the belief that students can collaborate effectively and that their classroom will be stronger for it. In Brian's classroom, pairs of students occupied a single table, regularly engaging in whatever activity he tossed out as a challenge.

On that particular day, I entered his room and immediately noticed something was different, and it wasn't hard to pinpoint the departure from the traditional: Unlike the vast majority of tables on the planet, the tables in his classroom that day were on their sides, the tabletops forming short walls snaking through the room.

The students were seated on the floor next to the overturned tables, writing furiously. They looked suspiciously like they were enjoying the process as well, which only added to my intrigue.

I wandered over to Brian, who was circulating the classroom, watching his students engage in this mysterious situation he had created.

"Hey, Rushton," he said as if we were chatting in the staff lounge, as opposed to a classroom where all the furniture had found new angles relative to the floor.

"Hey, Brian," I replied, following with the perfectly natural, "what's going on?"

"Oh, you see, it's World War I, and they're writing letters home from the trenches."

Beyond cool. Thunderously edu-awesome. Hope for learning, that is.

While I don't recall my time on that accreditation committee as anything life-changing, I doubt I'll ever forget seeing Brian's students as focused as they were that day in their "trenches."

Taking Brian's cue, how can we engage our students through activities while also helping them make new leaps in their understanding of our lesson's content? Is this kind of learning experience something that happens rarely or with frequency all over our schools? Shouldn't this kind of fascinating activity be the subject of at least a departmental discussion?

I believe that on every campus, every day that school is in session, something cool happens, big or small. Whether anyone takes notice is a different issue.

At your school, does the leader of each grade level, department, or leadership team regularly seek out examples of great learning moments? If so, how do they share them with the community?

One of the most common failings I've found in many American schools is the lack of an organized system for gathering success stories. It seems that far too often, in only the most extreme cases (a science fair winner, students having their writing published, a teacher winning a community award) is an academic-oriented or -leaning success identified and celebrated, and rarely are such successes carefully and creatively examined so other educators and students can replicate them.

In a world where it's easier than ever to gather and share information, though, why wouldn't schools look at stories like Brian's World War I lesson as successes to gather and share with the community?

This brings us back to the common barriers precluding our schools from developing exploratory cultures, one of those barriers being a professional culture that encourages keeping quiet about successes.

As educators have noted for years, teaching systems like those most commonly found in the United States tend to maximize time spent in front of classes and therefore minimize professional contact among educators, and this lack of professional interaction is one reason online communities have become such an important part of the lives of teachers now.

If you work in a school where teachers are regular, confident contributors to intellectually and professionally inspiring discussions, that's wonderful. However, I suspect the majority of you don't. In the last twenty-five years, I have met too many teachers who say they rarely, if ever, have these kinds of stimulating discussions within their schools' walls.

And having worked with and trained thousands of educators, I know very few of them, if given the choice, would choose to work in an environment in which their colleagues' individual successes remained hidden. Rather, they would prefer a setting in which everyone regularly explored how they could encourage one another to reach their full potential.

Arguably, a byproduct of this reluctance to share good news, interesting ideas, and cool possibilities is a conversational void too easily filled by complaints of poor student performance, poor facilities, poor leadership, or whatever else might occupy the dissatisfying side of someone's professional perspective.

The issue of why people complain is beyond the scope of our discussion, but I have no doubt that without much effort we can all think of several whiners among our colleagues. Without something else to fill the void, one gifted at complaint (and under the impression that their perspectives are shared by all) will surely step in with some grievance.

If my assumptions are correct, then the path forward may be to start with an agreement to try a new way of talking about possibilities for learning.

Improvement as a Point of Departure

Agreements start with shared truths.

Truth: Nothing that happens in a school (or anywhere else) is so good that improvement isn't possible.

Truth: Students can always push themselves to a higher level of intellectual curiosity and achievement. We will note that in some cases, higher level may not be our desired outcome; rather, it may be ethical development, organizational skills, interpersonal awareness, or another one of the student's pressing needs.

Truth: Parents can always partner more productively with a school to create better outcomes for their children and community as a whole. I've found families can offer valuable connections and ideas about the types of programs that might best serve their students and how to tap the talents of the teachers they have come to know. This statement is only true as long as parents perceive the work with their children's school representatives as a collaborative effort; likewise, the school's representatives must see their students' parents as helpful partners.

Truth: Teachers can always teach more effectively. I doubt even the best of us believe each and every one of our students is achieving at the very highest level and that nothing more is possible. The "best" teachers are actually more likely to be the ones always looking for a new tool, technique, or talent to reach more students and make them believe in what can happen when they push themselves.

Truth: Clerical staff can always take on a more effective role in improving their school's efficiency and introducing resources to their school's programs by using their systems and connections. For example, some schools' pressing need may be for the clerical team to use their knowledge of the systems in place to brainstorm ideas for teachers and campus leaders.

Truth: A school's leadership team must always look for and find ways to stay organized in their efforts to provide teachers new avenues for professional development, to better focus on their school's possibilities (rather than day-to-day fires), and to support both student- and teacher-led initiatives to foster new successes.

No matter your school's previous record of success, once everyone agrees improvement is a possibility, an easy next step is recognizing that some changes will be of value.

Start by understanding the power of the terminology you use. For example, you may notice that while everyone tends to be in favor of "improvement," you can encounter rather intense resistance if you were to use the term "change." Given that improvement, by definition, requires some level of change, we can address this logical problem with everyone involved by agreeing upon a framework (i.e., that improvement is possible) and then following steps that focus on what can or should be improved.

The hesitancy to make changes largely stems from a concern over time. A good start is identifying together those items for which the additional work of change is worth the possibility for improvement.

A detailed tool for this is "The Gripe Jam," a process Jennie Magiera coined in her impressive book, *Courageous Edventures: Navigating Obstacles to Discover Classroom Innovation*. In her book, Magiera walks us through the process of how a team can identify their concerns and then shift its focus to the most frustrating ones, those affecting the most people, and the ones team members are most passionate about solving. She then shows us how the team can identify approaches, stay focused on the strategy for addressing the problem, and even keep our eyes on the importance of celebrating whatever success comes from it.

Keep this in mind: However you choose to tackle your school's problems, both large and small, the exploration itself can be part of how the team grows together. That is to say, when considering a change—whether pursued or rejected—if everyone effectively listens to one another, by the end of the discussion, you may very well have a stronger team.

It is also worth noting that before setting off to develop success stories, both teachers and administrators need to understand that talking about their own victories is a requirement. In many settings, we think of this as "bragging," and the communication takes an unconstructive turn. However, given how common it is for educators of all descriptions to work on academic efforts individually, choosing only to discuss what we see others doing severely limits what we can identify and build upon.

I hope it's obvious by now, but how we talk about our successes is an important part of broadening them so they can benefit more students. That is to say, if when reporting your success, you come across as arrogant and annoying, it may be difficult for others to focus on those elements that made your work successful so they can build upon them to benefit their own students.

And it is equally problematic (and even more so, if systematized) when our colleagues, who are listening to our success stories, tend to assume that every report is necessarily the result of arrogance. The key in these discussions is for teachers to hear of successes, then adapt them to address the needs of their own students having trouble. These adaptations and their further exploration can allow everyone to take an activity to new levels of success.

Schools where teachers and administrators can comfortably talk about what goes well (and what doesn't) are places where everyone can regularly improve. In doing so, everyone can bring ideas to the classroom that may prove effective and almost certainly convey to students that their teacher is dedicated to their successes.

Success Discussions and Surveys

One way to foster the kind of exploration that focuses on creating a culture of examining and building upon success is to have a weekly team meeting, during which each person identifies a success from that week. The group takes the set of successes and brainstorms ideas for extending them.

The meeting starts with each person using a survey or collaboration tool to identify one success they've had since the last meeting. Over time, the team leader collects these successes as fodder for determining professional development goals, shaping collaboration time with other groups on campus, and developing the school's marketing materials.

Let's imagine a group of third-grade teachers using a Google Doc to identify the week's successes. They separate their successes into sections, following each success with questions from members on the grade-level team. The most useful questions go beyond a yes-no or single answer and leave room for further discussion.

Teacher 1: I used a voice recording app to have one of my struggling readers record and listen to a passage, then had her repeat the process as she heard herself improve. She was genuinely excited about hearing her progress because I don't think she actually realized she could improve.

- Which app did you use? Did the students have any difficulties with it that you had to overcome?

- Did you listen to the recording with the student and make suggestions, or did she work on this herself?

- Did you try this with other students? If so, did it work well for them, too?

Teacher 2: I had students work in pairs to write at least four captions for an image I showed them. Prompting the pairs to come up with several ideas resulted in more creative responses than when I had previously tried this activity and had each student create a single caption.

- How did you choose the image? Could the image have been part of the reason the answers were more creative?

- Did you give the students any strategies for brainstorming more ideas if they hit a block?

- Will the students use the captions for a future writing activity? If so, what?

Teacher 3: One of my students explained halves and quarters to the class using musical loops from Soundtrap (an online audio/music editing and creation tool). This was his first time to lead an activity, and the other students responded really well.

- How did he present what he'd learned? Did you give him choices for how to do the presentation?

- Can you review other concepts using the same tool, perhaps by using multiplication with beats and measures?

- If he created a song, how could you have the students create lyrics that draw connections with other things they're learning?

Teacher 4: As part of a history project, students pretended they were planning to build a town in a frontier region and had to talk about the kinds of places they would explore and what challenges they might face. They focused on the activity for more than an hour.

- Did the students come up with lists of possibilities themselves, or did they use a map tool or something similar to guide them?

- Could choices about what goes in the town reinforce some of the math they're learning?

- Were the students in groups, or did they have a full-class discussion? How did you keep some students from dominating the activity?

Note that in these examples, the teachers describe their successes in just two sentences. Limiting this brainstorming session to succinct descriptions does keep useful information from being included initially, but in so doing, gives the other teachers room to ask questions that could suggest alternate and potentially even more creative approaches.

Ultimately, we want to carefully and regularly gather success stories that can serve as points of departure for all sorts of possible avenues for improving learning activities.

One of the most important concepts I hope you take away from this book is that we must both pursue and also discuss success. In grade-level and department meetings, in staff meetings, in communications with the community, and in every other way possible, a school's leadership team must continually gather stories that show successes—what happens when students push themselves academically, when students show what it means to act compassionately, and when students use their creativity to help everyone see them and their possibilities in a new light.

Creating a Successes Survey

Collecting success stories is an important component of building an exploratory culture, and one can find many simple-to-use, free tools online, making it easy to create forms for gathering positive stories about a school or other organization. For our purposes, I will describe an approach using Google Forms, the survey tool in Google Drive.

We'll call our survey "The Success Survey," but your survey's name should match your team's character. So for your team, "What's Cool," "Cool Stuff at School," or "Making Me Proud" may be a better fit—go with whatever sings to you and your colleagues.

If you are new to survey tools, the idea is to create something online that anyone with an Internet-connected device—a laptop, tablet, smartphone, or similar—can quickly and easily access from wherever they are.

I suggest keeping the number of questions in your survey to a minimum—the longer a survey, the less likely someone is to take the time to fill it out.

In its most basic form, you will need these three pieces of information:

- The survey taker's name

- The person's contact information

- What struck the person as cool or as some sort of success

Which of the these components must be filled in before submitting the survey is up to the team gathering the stories, but obviously telling about the success is certainly the critical piece of information. If you anticipate a principal or team leader wanting to follow up to learn more about or verify the story, then the name and contact info would be good items to require.

So what kinds of success stories are you looking for? It could be from someone like me, who visited a colleague's classroom and saw a fascinating activity about World War I in action.

It could be from a student who saw a peer performing an act of kindness. Setting a positive tone starts by recognizing which acts are worth celebrating and then letting others know about them, after all.

It could be from a teacher who heard a particularly clever or creative comment in class. Creating an academic atmosphere that focuses on more than simply regurgitating facts is bolstered when we realize how often students really do share truly innovative insights, when given the avenues to do so.

It could be from a club advisor who was impressed by the extra effort the club's members put into a service activity. Building goodwill within the community is much easier when students help others beyond their campus. Students need to know they have something to give, and we must regularly cultivate the opportunities for them to do so.

The more the team identifies and celebrates all kinds of successes, the more quickly and easily team members will share what they see. We'll explore this idea further when we look at staff meetings, but first let's begin with how the survey can work with PR efforts.

Sharing Successes

Using Google Forms, all of the information your team members submit is easily collected in a spreadsheet, which you can then share with the people focused on your school's or program's PR efforts. This PR team should regularly review the survey's entries, sharing the best items to your school's or program's public-facing website, social media pages, or blog, creating a steady stream of good news that both encourages the community and inspires students and teachers.

Even though PR should be an integral component to discussions about campus atmosphere, staff morale, and student pride, in my travels I've encountered remarkably few schools with an organized public relations plan. Sometimes the school's leadership team just doesn't believe there is a need for one because they don't see themselves as competing with other schools for students. Sometimes the leadership feels no one has time to devote to the effort.

Setting aside the increasing competition homeschooling and online options pose to traditional education, a strong PR plan's importance does not necessarily lie in marketing efforts and fending off competition; rather, it affects how the school's community supports its team members' efforts, along with how the teaching staff pushes itself to create the best professional environment possible.

So if regularly sharing stories leads to focusing on activities that then create more stories worth sharing, how can a school help its stakeholders and supporters within the community use these stories to strengthen how they think about the school?

To start, let's note that traditional approaches to sharing information are still of value in this situation.

If your school sends a physical newsletter home to parents, use the accelerated production of success stories to your advantage and make them front-page fodder.

If your school puts out press releases to local media outlets, make sure that they always include links to where your team collects and tells the stories of your school.

If you have an online newsletter, reaching more community members requires minimal effort. Add an explicit request that recipients share these stories with others.

If your school has parent evenings, such as a back-to-school night, use digital media tools (videos, online presentation tools, narrated slideshows, and the like) to share stories with attendees, who can then share them with other parents who couldn't attend.

If your school has created short videos talking about your stories of success, regularly send them to your email lists and post them to social media. You'll find that when something is easily shareable, it is great for building the community's pride in the school.

One of my favorite examples of a school using one of its successes to tell about itself is a parent involvement effort by Easterbrook Discovery School (EDS), a K-8 school in San Jose, California. Although EDS is a public school, parents choose it for their children because of its focus on collaborative and project-based learning. Among the school's many strengths is the annual outreach program to students' fathers and father figures called "Dads and Dudes on Duty."

Each year, students' dads or "special dudes" (uncles, grandfathers, and other mentors) visit the school so they can see firsthand their children's classrooms, meet other fathers and special dudes, have some coffee, and generally get to know the school.

Watch the video that one of the EDS team members, John Lozano, created telling the "Dads and Dudes on Duty" story at NextVista.org/dads-and-dudes.

In just three minutes, we see images and footage

of students enjoying learning and playing with their fathers and special dudes, interviews with these men talking about what it means to them to have the opportunity to be at the school, and footage showing the day's very positive atmosphere.

These men's stories of how they get to take part in their children's learning activities is visually powerful, and hearing the men and their children recite the EDS pledge reminds us how the school sees itself:

> *We are the EDS Huskies.*
> *Every day, we listen, learn, and laugh.*
> *We are responsible, respectful, and cooperative.*
> *We promise to take care of our school and our world.*
> *We believe in ourselves and never give up.*
> *Believe it!*

The piece is touching in many ways. Every school works to involve parents in their children's education, and most find it especially challenging to get their students' male role models actively involved. Almost anyone watching the video would agree that EDS nailed it.

This is a beautiful story that those who watch will want to share. It's short, it makes the viewer feel good about the school, and it's in an easily-shared form.

The most powerful piece of the video for me is the very last line. As the music finishes, "Dads and Dudes on Duty—an event every school should have" appears on the screen.

It is no small thing to assert that what your school is doing is something schools everywhere should do. But as we think about what makes our schools special, at the top of that list should be anything that our school's team is so passionate about that we would want every school's students to have the same opportunity.

Think about it this way: "What we're doing is so good for kids, we want every child, everywhere, to have a day like this each year."

Working Backward from the Story to the Activity

Whether the story you want to tell about your school is a fine-tuned celebration of student possibilities, is on its way to being so, or merely a gleam in your eye, first think about the story itself and then work toward how you will share it.

I'm sure those of you familiar with backward design approaches for crafting curriculum will see the parallels almost immediately. That's because when we shift from creating effective curricula to creating effective PR practices, we are still focusing on asking critical questions about goals and then determining the best way to reach those identified goals.

What visuals (images or footage) would someone need in order to understand, and even feel, the importance of the activity or program you're highlighting? What would cause these moments of understanding to take place? Who would record them? What would you need in place for your success to become compellingly visible? Have you and your team brainstormed all the components of this project, factoring in what could go wrong and how you would handle complications? Have you, as a team, learned how to talk through ideas about how the story might be told?

Ideally, anyone watching the video you ultimately create would immediately understand (without having to learn any "edu-jargon") what your students are doing, why it's important, and how your school has made the opportunity a vibrant one for participants.

Clearly, for sharing stories in ways that are both compelling and easy to assemble, your team will need to wrap its collective mind around the idea of sharing stories using video, and this leads to several pieces of advice.

First, keep videos short. Videos lasting no more than two minutes are more likely to be watched all the way to the end, viewed multiple times, and shared with others.

Second, your video's quality does not have to be amazing, but it should have clear audio. Being willing to go back and record something more than once is a nice reminder that striving for quality is normally more important than finishing quickly. There are times when striving for quality makes the process interminable. When you think you might be going down that road, then, in the words of the famous poster, "Done is better than perfect."

Third, invite those who watch your video to share their thoughts on it so you can improve your videos going forward. This can be a good way to draw people into taking an active part in your school's community. And while it's entirely possible that someone will be an annoyingly frequent critic, that's a far better problem to have than the community not knowing your stories.

Fourth, a smartphone is a perfectly good tool to record footage with, but hold your phone horizontally, not vertically. For more details on the dangers of this issue, watch the video "Vertical Video Syndrome" on

YouTube.[1] Again, keep squarely in mind that you should have good audio quality.

Fifth, consider supporting your students' parents who have limited English ability by either adding subtitles to your video or creating a translated version. (Note: Google Translate, while a good tool for working with a parent face-to-face, is *not* a substitute for having someone who can actually read and write the language prepare a script for subtitles or narration.)

I could go on, but ultimately, everything comes down to these questions: Do your students and colleagues really like the video you made? If not, can they offer you suggestions for how to improve it? If they can, are you willing to act upon their suggestions? This is good modeling for how we teach, of course.

You may also ask each teacher on your team to look for something each quarter or semester that can become one of the school's stories, and then begin building a team of teachers and/or students to capture these stories as videos. If your school's staff embraces the idea, you could end up with a strong library of evidence of your school's efforts.

---

[1] Rimes, Ben. "Vertical Video Syndrome (Clean Version)" YouTube video. 2:17. Posted November 20, 2014. https://www.youtube.com/watch?v=f2picMQC-9E

Spreading the Love(ly Ideas)

Sharing ideas with one another can lead to activities that become new stories of success, which is why it is so important for each of us to talk about our successes. While many teachers have a tendency to try to shut down these kinds of conversations, you can sway the reluctant as you seek to turn the tide in the positive direction at your school using the following arguments and approaches.

To begin, when we tell our story from our perspective and focus on what we did, it can sound a lot like the bragging that can shut down productive sharing. But if we instead tell our success story from our students' standpoint and describe what they did, the topic becomes more comfortable. After all, the teacher can make something great happen in the classroom, but the real evidence of success lies in what the students do.

Next, with today's freely available tools, we can easily share our stories with other schools near and far, allowing us to show one another new ways to reach those students who have been stubbornly resistant to embracing their potential.

You may want to make this kind of sharing part of a larger argument for helping reluctant educators become comfortable with constructive, creative conversations, but it could also help you better understand the value your successes offer your colleagues and their students. After all, as the "Dads and Dudes Duty" video reminded us, why shouldn't we strive to do our job so that it benefits students all over the world?

To build your network of sharing, whenever you attend conferences and district trainings, begin developing contacts who reliably communicate their schools' successes with you and who are comfortable giving you ideas on the stories you share with them. Ideally, these colleagues will be comfortable receiving feedback about what doesn't work and more than happy to share what does. The hope is that everyone has a sense of pride in extending their successes to reach more students in need of creative approaches.

Expanding Realms of Success

When we think of what success is, we tend to limit ourselves to past events; however, success stories worth celebrating can also be found in the now and the not-yet.

Take, for example, the smile on a student's face when they finish a project and compliments are flying their way. Obviously, that is a success story, but what about the excitement that a student experiences when powerfully memorable learning kicks into gear? Consider when a project captures a student's imagination, when students focus all of their attention on what they are learning, when they are oozing curiosity, and when the path forward is illuminated just enough to intrigue them. All of these are successes.

The video game industry has known this for years. Gamers are intrigued to figure out the puzzles and challenges that they encounter. They are on the lookout for hints as to what awaits them at every turn. They collaborate with others to make progress. They work constantly to add new tools and talents they can bring to their quests. As they play the games, not only are they not distracted, but they understand the negative effects of being distracted. They understand that they will experience all sorts of failure on their way to mastering the game.

Exactly where the power of gaming sits for education and learning is a vibrant discussion in education circles. Researchers like Jane McGonigal in the San Francisco Bay Area have explored the many positive possibilities of gaming. Educators like Lucas Gillispie and Peggy Sheehy have shared their ideas and experiments through blogs and speaking with thousands of teachers.

That there are important ideas in this industry, which by some accounts has surpassed movies and music in terms of revenue, is not in question.

Whether we will use such ideas to enhance our professional experiences in the near term is, however. This is about more than engaging students; it's about making what we explore with colleagues a more active piece of our work. Let's consider this by turning to one area of our work well past ripe for pushing reset: the staff meeting.

The Staff Meeting, Evolved

For many teachers, the staff meeting is the most common setting for professional interaction. It is also reviled as tedium that borders on torture. One saying goes this way: "If I die, I hope it's during a staff meeting, because the transition to death would be so subtle."

While presenting at a summit in Mumbai several years ago, though, I got into a conversation with one teacher about her school in Delhi, and happened to ask about their staff meetings.

"Oh, they're great!" she offered, with no eye-rolling or other sign that she was pushing the sarcasm meter past the red.

"Your staff meetings are great?" I asked.

"Yes, I always get there early to get a good seat."

"We're talking about your staff meetings, right?"

"Yes. We call them 'The Bob Show.'"

She went on to explain that their superintendent, an inspired soul named Bob, had only a handful of these meetings each year. They wouldn't cover announcements, but instead would watch short videos that would elicit laughter and tears, and then work together to explore ideas related to the videos and what they could mean for the school.

I'll admit that, while I've never met Bob, from that moment forward, I've had a pretty serious man-crush on him.

So how can we too use exciting ideas to shift our staff meetings from dull to engaging? To start with, let's note that at the meetings the teacher from Delhi described, teachers *do* things.

One way is to start your staff meeting by having everyone fill out your school's "Success Survey" (or whatever you call your survey). This could be done during grade-level or departmental meetings as well, but ensuring everyone has time to share what is going on at the school is important, and the beginning of the staff meeting is a good opportunity to make that happen.

As the "Success Survey" becomes a regular habit at meetings, you will probably notice your colleagues looking for stories of success in anticipation of the next meeting.

After everyone completes their survey, have someone share several of the items from the previous staff meeting's survey and invite those familiar with each success to add details about what students have done or are doing to paint a clearer picture of the story. Anyone interested would know that person is the one to approach to get more detail, and the stronger the conversations that arise out of these quick sharing moments, the better the team gets.

Sharing good stories at the outset of a staff meeting sets a tone that makes what follows all the more positive and productive. Follow up the survey with activities that challenge the group to see new possibilities for themselves and the students.

Imagine that after focusing the first ten to fifteen minutes on the "Cool Stuff at School" survey and its responses from the previous meeting, the staff were then to form groups spanning grade levels, departments, and offices. Having this variety in each group lets everyone have the chance to hear from colleagues doing different kinds of work and ensures everyone gains new perspectives on their own efforts. They could work with ideas from videos like the teachers in Delhi did or try something even more active, such as the potential offered by free technologies.

The groups can then use a set of links to free technologies to explore new possibilities for learning activities. Along the way, they can become better attuned to how students with fewer financial resources might use these to stay up to speed with their peers.

Give each group a list of free technologies (you could use "Even More" from Google or NextVista.org's Resources pages) and have each group identify one item that is new to them. Next, groups should spend five to ten minutes coming up with at least three crazy ideas for how they could use that technology to help students. Teams can capture their ideas using sticky notes or a free brainstorming tool like Padlet (Padlet.com). Out of these crazy ideas can come some amazing innovations.

The 20Time Project author Kevin Brookhouser does something similar with his students. He has found that getting them to loosen up and engage in what he calls "The Bad Idea Factory" leads them to think practically about how to make something different happen while brainstorming, along with a freedom to suggest some "out-there" possibilities. The idea is to come up with bad ideas, and the fact that good ones also find their way into the discussion is a happily natural byproduct.

Ultimately, this is an exercise in creativity. The idea is to help all members of the team understand that they have something to contribute to the discussion, no matter how much technology they know or don't know. I would even recommend having the activity leader explicitly tell the team, "If you're not having fun with this, you're not doing it right."

You could do this activity multiple times to expose team members to a variety of tools and also mix up the teams so more connections are made among the staff. Once everyone's ideas have been collected, give folks time to see the suggestions. Hopefully, this will result in some friendly laughter and at least a few people saying, "That might be worth trying!"

Done well, this kind of exploration can move staff meetings from drudgery (leadership makes announcements that could have been sent via email) to a philosophical place where team members celebrate the success of generating new ideas, and share an interest in and enthusiasm for giving these ideas a try.

I hope these ideas paint a clearer picture of what a school with an exploratory culture looks like and the kinds of activities these educators regularly engage in. What individual team members are willing to share and do, though, requires confidence—confidence that dares to explore what makes an educator of any description someone who can be recognized as a true professional. To that, we turn next.

Chapter 5

Individual Confidence

I s teaching different today than it was decades
ago?

While much about schools hasn't changed,
the personal and professional experiences of the teachers within them have evolved in profound ways, thanks
in large part to the advent of the Internet.

If the bulk of studies looking at how long teachers
stay in the profession are to be believed then between
7.4 and 8.4 percent of U.S. teachers leave the profession
every year. (See statistics from the US Department of
Education,[1] this report from the National Education
Association,[2] or this news piece from NPR.[3]) These edu-

---

[1] "Research Spotlight on Recruitment and Retention," National Education Association, accessed January 10, 2017, http://www.nea.org/tools/16977.htm.

[2] "Research Spotlight on Recruitment and Retention," National Education Association, accessed January 10, 2017, http://www.nea.org/tools/16977.htm.

[3] "Revolving Door Of Teachers Costs Schools Billions Every Year," NPR, accessed January 10, 2017, http://www.npr.org/sections/ed/2015/03/30/395322012/the-hidden-costs-of-teacher-turnover.

cators cite such concerns as isolation and feeling like they don't have other adults whom they can turn to for ideas, resources, and encouragement.

Today, however, isolation has become less a function of our profession and more to do with a teacher's lack of sophistication using readily available resources.

Thanks to the Internet, we have ready and regular access to educators who share our passion for innovative approaches to teaching a subject, helping in the community, serving students with specific backgrounds and challenges, and sharing hobbies of all descriptions. Easily created professional learning networks make commiserating, brainstorming, and celebrating with others easy.

No longer are thoughts about possibilities for improvement locked into the spatial limitations of a single campus or an infrequently attended local group of professionals. Now, if you want to try something, with a quick web search, you will likely find others already giving it a go. In other words, if you are confident that innovation is integral to the best kinds of teaching and learning, I promise you, there has never been a better time to be a teacher.

Saving Time

Consider, for example, what most teachers would identify as their biggest stressor: limited time.

Any dedicated teacher likely spends hours upon hours creating and doing research for each lesson's plans and resources, especially if the topic is unfamiliar. Unfortunately, this preparation can take up valuable time that could be better spent determining alternative approaches to a lesson, particularly if those non-traditional approaches would benefit students needing something different.

If you are not all that familiar with technology, one of the best ways you can begin dipping your toes in is to learn how to access resources other teachers have created about your topic and adapt their materials for your own purposes. After all, anything that both gives you a promising idea and saves you time is worth a good look.

Mcet James, a seventh-grade teacher preparing his first lesson on haiku poetry. He has been tasked with addressing the topic as one of the curriculum's standards, but he has no real experience with Japanese culture or literature, and has a hunch that having been to a sushi restaurant once won't prove a major help.

One way he could see how other teachers have presented haiku is by doing a web search for "haiku poetry," "haiku poetry middle school," or similar. (We'll use Google as our tool for this example, but if something better comes along, use that instead.)

Web searches can turn up some interesting sites, but they may also include results without any direct relevance to your immediate need, which, in James' case, is presenting haiku to his students.

If James were to drop the following search query in Google's search field, however, he may get notably better results:

haiku poetry introduction filetype:ppt

The "filetype:ppt" code directs Google to return only results that are PowerPoint files, not web pages. While PowerPoint lacks many of the visual features newer presentation tools offer, it does have the advantage of having been around for a geologic age in Internet time as well as hordes upon hordes of people who have created content with it.

Looking at his search results, James can zero in on the web addresses (URLs) to see if helpful pointers such as "k12" appear, allowing him to determine which ones to examine first.

When I did this search, the first result was a set of slides featuring easy-to-understand definitions, examples tied to common themes in haiku, and even a set of pictures serving as prompts for students to write haiku themselves.

If James found the same presentation, he might decide that he now has a wonderful point of departure and can adapt the slides to fit whichever presentation tool with which he is most comfortable. To model good digital citizenship for his students, he also makes sure to cite who created the slides and where he found them.

Similarly, let's consider Laura, who learns a week before school starts that she will be teaching an environmental science class. Unfortunately, the facts that (a) she has never taught such a class and (b) no textbook is available didn't dissuade the person in charge of the high school's master schedule from assigning it to her.

Rather than freezing with panic or wallowing in misery at a local bar, Laura types the following into Google's search field:

high school environmental science syllabus filetype:pdf

She downloads four or five of the most promising hits (these will all be PDF files, which are documents designed to open in multiple online environments and operating systems) and quickly gets an idea of how other teachers have approached arranging the course's main topics.

Laura may not be happy about the added challenge to her year, but under the circumstances, she does have what she needs to get a much stronger start than she would have otherwise.

Simply adding "filetype:ppt" to your web searches (or using the features on the advanced search page, if you are comfortable doing so) may very well save you dozens of hours of work over the course of a school year; however, the possibilities with this one-word-and-one-colon tool don't stop with saving time.

While searching for PowerPoint presentations, you will probably come across some pretty bad ones. Perhaps the slides include irrelevant images, don't clearly and concisely present the information, or have spelling and grammar issues, or maybe the creator didn't go to the trouble of citing any sources.

Finding bad presentations may sound like an inconvenience, but I'd suggest that it represents an opportunity. Rather than dismissing these presentations as useless and moving on, you could ask your students about a week into your unit to get in groups and take a look at the bad presentation and explain what's wrong with it.

At first, this search technique may seem like manna from beyond, but eventually, you'll face a sobering realization: students can also use the same approach when tasked with creating a presentation. They may do this dishonorably, changing only the presentation creator's name and suggesting that it is actually their work (an uncool, but fairly common move, this is).

"He's right! I wondered why that kid had included the word 'oleaginous' in his presentation!"

Yes, there are students who cheat using technology. This isn't likely to be a surprise to you.

Of course, any time you suspect a presentation isn't a student's original work, you can do the filetype search with either the title or an uncommon phrase or word appearing on one of the slides, and it may well show up as one of the first few hits. Plagiarists are, by definition, lazy.

Rather than focusing on proof of wrongdoing by our wayward student, you could reconsider the nature and value of the assignment itself.

If your students have been learning about Imperial China, asking each one to come up with a presentation about the Great Wall may result in a number of tediously similar efforts.

Another approach would be to announce this assignment:

"Okay, everyone, we've spent the last two weeks studying Imperial China. So, for next Wednesday, I want you to pair up, then find and download three presentations about the Great Wall. For each one, explain what you see as its strengths, identify its weaknesses, explore how we would validate the information it presents, and explain how you would have put that presentation together differently."

Ideally, this would encourage your students to both shift into a frame of mind for thinking about higher-quality work and to consider how they evaluate the ocean of digital media they swim in daily.

Sharing the results of such an activity with a professional network can result in more suggestions you can experiment with, and you may be offering a new possibility to them as well. Learning that we are professionals who have something to offer can be a great help in building our confidence.

Comparative Confidence

The filetype trick for finding what's readily available is not merely to save you some time. For those of you who you find technology intimidating (and you are far from alone), simple techniques like using "filetype" in your searches may allow you to say to yourself, "Hmmm ... I think I could do *that*."

Even for those of us with mountains of technology experience, taking on something new can be a battle waged with both time and psychology. We have covered the time part at some length, but the psychology part, at least in the context of our discussion, may be new.

Wanting to become familiar with settings, textbooks, techniques, resources, and tools is a natural goal. The less time we spend navigating the unfamiliar, the more time we can devote to interacting with our students, pondering what occupies our horizons, or simply having the cat chase the laser pointer.

That familiarity, though, can quickly morph into an initially inconspicuous stagnation. It starts when we begin choosing the familiar path—not because our students need it, but because it is easy for us. Under our

---

Familiarity can quickly morph into an initially inconspicuous stagnation.

---

radar, the more we continue making the easy choice, the less confident we become in our ability to try something new.

Those of us teaching in isolation can find it all the more difficult to ignore the seductive whisper of the demon of comfort. We walk into our classrooms and—by doing a passable, if rather tediously boring, job of presenting our topics—we move along without ever bringing unwanted attention to ourselves.

However, as I have hinted before, settling for lackluster can deprive us of the best kinds of experiences and much of the fun we can have as teachers, such as when our students treat us to unexpected insights and enthusiasm. Unexpected insights and enthusiasm can be good grist for great stories of what makes a school special, as well!

The transition from developed fluency, to comfortable facility, to relying upon the easy, to weakened confidence about our own ability to improve. In fact, it can happen so slowly that once we realize where depleted confidence has brought us, we fear we've irrevocably lost the mojo we had when we were regularly adding to our tool belt.

I'd argue this realization probably won't come to us as a simple moment of clarity on the way to work. I think it is more likely to happen when we see a colleague trying something impressive, and the thought that "Wow, I haven't done something new in a long time!" hits us. Only then might it dawn on us that deep inside, we're afraid to try the same activity ourselves.

Rediscovering the fun that comes from our work is far from impossible. In fact, a natural byproduct of connecting with educators beyond our local colleagues is that our self-imposed limitations diminish. That's because when we only focus on the few examples we see each day, it becomes too easy to think, "I can't do what that person does."

In some cases, this may be true—what one teacher does may be so tied to his or her personality that emulation is impossible. But in most cases, we unintentionally ignore the wealth of possibilities that can come from combining our own strengths with aspects of what makes our colleague and their activity so successful.

In beginning to understand this possibility for developing our own singular strengths, we turn the tide against what I call, "CIS," or "Comparative Inadequacy Syndrome."

What is CIS? Well, it's tragically common among teachers. It's a malady that eats away at the very soul of those who suffer from it. It's what transforms strong, promising teachers into weak ones, bit by depressing bit.

Is it real? Yes. Now, admittedly, I made it up, but it does reflect something horribly real.

Simply put, CIS is the tendency we have to focus on what we cannot do rather than what we might try.

It's looking at others and deciding we cannot replicate their successes.

It leads to our holding ourselves back from taking advantage of the strengths we have developed through years or decades of hard work, all out of fear that we have been passed up. At its worst, CIS results in our giving up on what we might accomplish, though this is easily avoided if only we were to have a little more confidence in who and what we are.

Students profess this kind of worry as well. You hear it in statements like, "I can't do what all the other kids can do!"

Never mind that "all the other kids" are really just a few successful members of the group and that the student strangling himself with self-doubt is more the rule than the exception.

I have been discussing CIS at conferences for several years now because it always leads me to share a special thought that has the potential to not only turn around someone's confidence, but also accelerate the shedding of their self-doubt while quickly building excitement for what they might try that day and going forward.

What is that thought? It's this:

The only person to whom you ever need compare yourself is the you who you were yesterday.

The only person to whom you ever need compare yourself is the you who you were yesterday.

In other words, every single day, we can take a new idea, a new tool, or a new technique and see how using it could help our students.

The simple message, "Guys, today, we're going to try something new!" conveys an enthusiasm for the unknown that we might hope to inculcate in the students who happen to find themselves in our classes.

Many of our students have difficulty moving forward out of fear they will not be successful. Trying, and sometimes failing, is a more powerful way of letting them know that none of us is perfect—nor is there reason for people to expect that we ever will be. That's a lesson for both them, and us, as well.

I believe this realization can also result in plenty of fun for us *and our students.*

Ask your students what they think of something you've tried. Was the tool or activity useful for their learning? If trying it again, how could it be altered to make it more effective?

Students do know something about school and learning—after all, it is where and how they spend a major portion of their time. So I think you'll find they are pleasantly surprised when you are willing to tap their ideas.

Common Experiences

I consider myself a wildly fortunate person, and not just because my very best friend agreed to spend her life with me.

I'm fortunate because I have the opportunity to work with teachers all over the world. I visit huge schools, and I visit schools with only a handful of students. I have seen schools where expectations are off the charts for everyone, and I have seen schools where teachers have given up on the very students they are supposed to serve. I have worked with teachers with all manner of resources available to them, and I have worked with teachers to whom many of the basics are appallingly unavailable.

In every school I visit, though, people have three common concerns that stand in their way of trying new things:

- Do I know enough about this technique or technology to try it? Won't I need to master it before making it part of my practice?

- Why do we have to change anything? What I've done has been successful for a long time.

- What if the students know more than I do about what we're using? Won't I look foolish to them? Won't I look foolish to my colleagues for giving it a try?

And while these issues are complex for many reasons, their solutions are not.

- We can't master anything unless we give it a try, and when students learn that we want to develop new ways of helping them, their confidence in us grows.

- We change simply because we think we can improve, and we do so for our students' benefit.

This doesn't mean shelving what has been successful. On the contrary, it means adapting it so we can meet the needs of more students than we have helped in the past.

- Students may know more about how to use a tool than we do, but their knowledge is almost always limited to the one way they want to use it. Ask a good question about how else one could use it, and all of a sudden, you are learning *with* your student, which could lead to a life-changing moment for them.

Earlier, I mentioned my high school chemistry teacher, Mr. Plyler.

He took an interest in us and asked us about the things we were seeking to learn and become. This wasn't something creepy; how he communicated let us know he believed in our ability to realize our possibilities. He talked *with* us rather than *at* us.

Mr. Plyler knew I was interested in learning BASIC computer programming language. Those of you who are my age-ish perhaps recall it:

```
10 print "I am stuck in a loop."
20 goto 10
```

I've probably forgotten enough syntax to make even that effort questionable.

At the time, I had an Apple II+, and I would use it to type up and run simple programs when I wasn't playing tennis, hanging out with friends, trying to get a girl to pay attention to me, or watching *Star Trek*.

One of the challenges of working with variables in BASIC, and many programming languages for that matter, is successfully creating what's called a "bubble sort." This is when the program takes a set of terms (for example, the numbers one to ten); chooses one at random; removes it from the list; takes another randomly selected number from those remaining; makes it the next item in the new set; and in a series of operations equal to the number of items in the set (ten, in this example), the program creates a randomized version of the first set.

I couldn't figure it out.

I tried, and failed, and tried again, and failed again. I then tried again, and failed yet again. I was stuck in a loop.

One afternoon, after becoming rather fed up with not getting my bubble sort program to work, I tried it a totally different way, mostly out of exasperation.

It worked. I nearly fell over I was so excited.

The next morning before school started, I zipped straight to Mr. Plyler's classroom.

"Hey, Mr. Plyler, I figured it out! I figured it out!"

"Really?" he replied. "What did you do?"

I enthusiastically began to explain my code.

"Hmmm … I'm not getting it. Why don't you put it on the board?"

So I did, writing it all and explaining each bit as I went.

While I was doing this, another student walked into the room and came over to Mr. Plyler to get his attention.

After she approached and began asking him a question, he turned to her and said, "Hold on a minute, I'm learning something."

I stopped writing and looked back. He was learning from me. I was someone who could teach an adult. Wow.

I went back to my explanation, but I never went back to who I was before that moment.

Mr. Plyler didn't really know much about programming, but he was curious, and he enjoyed learning cool stuff.

He also had no problem letting me know that he didn't know, and in so doing, he gave me an image of myself I hadn't had before I walked into his classroom that morning.

In summary, don't worry about what you don't know. Simply show you are interested in what your students think and that you are willing to learn from them. In doing so, you may change a life. That life may change another life. And so on.

Good loop, that.

Notes on Learning

As we become more confident in our ability to try new things, sooner or later we will probably come face to face with assumptions about our setting and work that require a rather significant departure from what we have done before.

Let's work with an example that I consider a doozy. That is, let's talk about notes and note-taking.

It may not sound particularly doozy-esque, but notes are a critical component for student success in everything beyond elementary school. What's more, the weaknesses we can see in how students typically take and understand their notes offer an interesting opportunity to experiment with newer technologies.

Let me start by mentioning how I normally present this idea to teachers:

Some time ago, I was looking for an image that captured the idea of "bad notes." I started where I always start, the Creative Commons search page (search.creativecommons.org/); searched for the term "bad notes"; and up popped this image by Kate Brady:

Bad Notes by Kate Brady from Flickr (CC by 2.0)
https://www.flickr.com/photos/cliche/4437609364.

At the top of this lined page that any late twentieth-century student (and many now) would use are the words "All about Wildfires."

I think it's perfect—that is, it's the perfect example of how I worry students take notes. A half-dozen or so thoughts are only tenuously related to one another, and at the top and on the side are drawings of all sorts of monsters. Somewhat down the page is the rather daunting biological observation, "We're all going to die."

I've certainly felt that way in a class before, and I'm sure there have been students in my classroom wondering if the end-of-class bell would ring before some apocalyptic meteor with good aim—proving inconvenient for the continuance of life on the planet, but admittedly mercifully timed—would arrive and bring an end to what they were enduring at that very moment.

Anyway, plenty of students have trouble taking good notes. Imagine that some young soul listening to the teacher hears a new term and decides to write the word down. The student may not be able to spell it, and after musing on possible vowel combinations for a moment, goes with a guess, only looking up to find that the teacher is now a sentence or two past the point when the word was first mentioned.

So the student is now trying to associate what the teacher is saying with the word whose spelling was just mangled in epic fashion, minus whatever useful thoughts were uttered during the spelling challenge.

Now imagine the student is convinced that what the teacher is now presenting is critically important. Why? Because this teacher is writing the sentence on the board. Clear giveaway, that move.

So our student carefully writes down the sentence, which takes some time because writing is not something the child tends to do unless forced to, and once the final punctuation is applied, our kiddo realizes the teacher has said another four to six sentences' worth of material. More confusion associated with the disparate items ensues.

The student may then ask a question, the answer for which was just made explicitly clear by the teacher. Our teacher may show some frustration and comment on the student's lack of attention, which teaches the student that asking questions is a surefire way to make the entire room think you are stupid. The solution is simple: stop asking questions.

I could go on and factor in those students having trouble paying attention, but I think I've made my point.

As I see it, the real miracle is that some students take notes well.

So when do we teach students how to take good notes?

Let's ask some college professors.

"They should learn that in high school."

Let's check with the high school teachers.

"I believe that's covered in middle school."

Let's check with the middle school teachers.

"That's a skill taught in fourth and fifth grade, right?"

You get the idea. Unless students are in a program like AVID,[4] chances are good that no one has ever tried teaching them *how* to take notes. And when would they have had the chance to watch someone else do it? I'm guessing never-ish.

If what I've described is accurate for any number of students, those for whom the description fits probably find it a cruel joke when a teacher suggests that the next exam will be "open notes." Here comes that feeling of "We're all going to die."

So what do we do?

Imagine for a moment that you are the teacher, and that you have a class full of students, each possessing an Internet-connected device. Let's also assume you know

---

[4] http://www.avid.org

how to use Google Docs or a similar online collaboration tool.

You say: "Alright class, we're getting ready to start Unit Five. I've created a new doc for the notes and shared it with all of you. Teresa, today you'll be the primary notetaker, and, Jonathan, you'll be secondary. Everyone else, if you choose you can have your device open with a page for the currently, but not-for-long, blank doc that will get these notes. Either way, your main job is to pay attention."

The lesson goes forward, with Teresa adding everything she can to the notes document, but not worrying much about details, as Jonathan cleans up her additions as they go. Students can see the notes Teresa and Jonathan are taking, but they do not have to take notes themselves.

With ten minutes left in class, you stop and project the students' notes to the front of the room.

"Alright, everyone. Let's think back to what stood out for each of you over the course of the lesson. Did everything that needed to become part of the notes make it into the document?"

Now you are reviewing the lesson's main topics with the class, and you can ask students why an idea seemed important enough that it should be added to the notes.

This may help many students become familiar with the clues that a good note-taker notices all the time, while gaining a sense of how different students are reacting to the lesson's various ideas.

I want to emphasize that going back over the day's notes is in no way a "Gotcha!" for Teresa and Jonathan, who are also learning from this exercise through the review. The message to convey is that we are all, at all times, learning from one another, and by cleaning up the doc at the end of each class, we want to make sure everyone has a good set of notes from which to study.

Each day, the primary and secondary note-takers change, and there may be some students with such weak skills that they are never the primary person. On those days when they are secondary, make sure you have a particularly strong primary notetaker.

I can imagine how some of my former colleagues would react to this exercise: "That's ridiculous! It's spoon-feeding students rather than requiring them to do what they'll need to succeed in college."

While I agree that spoon-feeding is normally counter-productive, I'd argue that letting bad note-takers continue to be bad without any guidance on how to improve isn't doing anything to prepare them for whatever might be next.

Will a note-taking system like the one I've described work for every teacher and every class? Of course not. Not all schools have the wifi infrastructure required to allow students to share an online document. It's possible some students would sabotage the notes just to be troublesome. It's also possible students believe their teacher will respond to their questions with sarcasm, poisoning the waters for meaningful discussion before any speaking begins. Students may have note-taking skills at levels that would make this unnecessary.

The important thing is that to whatever extent we try something like this, we must make sure it's seen by all as part of a shared attempt to find what works for everyone.

Because when we have the confidence to try something new, when we see what we do in our classrooms as exploratory, and when we make a continuous effort to identify and use our tools alongside students' and colleagues' talents, we reveal promising possibilities for everyone.

Confidence that motivates one to act on an idea can prove an elusive challenge for both students and teachers. So when we offer encouragement and make clear what constitutes big and small successes, we help our classes and colleagues begin to see their new possibilities. And when we act upon the next idea, become comfortable with making adjustments as we go, and develop a pattern of academic and professional accomplishment, we create the perfect conditions for personal success.

And schools filled with personal successes are clearly special places to learn and work.

Chapter 6
What We Should Do

It was the late 1990s, and I was teaching high school Japanese language on the east side of San Jose, California. My students spanned geographic and ethnic spectra, meaning every period felt like a mini United Nations was assembling in my classroom. And though the students' backgrounds were varied, they were all united by one driving interest:

An intense desire for academic achievement?

No.

The drive to make their families and sensei proud every day?

No.

The vast majority of my students entered the program not out of a sense this was their path to Harvard, or with the goal of starting the next trans-Pacific mega-corporation.

What united these teens was (wait for it…) a love of Japanese animation.

"Are we going to watch cartoons in this class?" some excited first-year student would breathlessly ask me on the first day of school.

"No, but we're going to do tons of homework!" I'd reply with a similar enthusiasm.

Then I'd let the students know they were on the path to reading and uttering stuff that few around them could imagine themselves capable of, and that I was glad to have the opportunity to share with them the Japanese language—something that has struck me as fascinatingly cool ever since I began learning it in 1987.

And I would tell them that, yes, if they put in the effort, what they learned in my class would allow them to understand their beloved cartoons in a whole new way.

One day, sometime in 1999-ish, I was winding down a lesson in a Japanese 1 class, and we had about ten minutes left, exactly the time I had set aside for a short quiz.

"Okay, guys, clear your desks. Keep out just a pencil and an eraser."

They did so, and I distributed the quiz, finishing with my standard pre-quiz and pre-test exhortation: "Make me proud!"

The students went to work, their heads hovering over their quizzes as I walked the classroom, hoping my proximity would help them decide against the dishonorable path of looking for answers on their peers' papers.

The students finished up, I collected the papers, and the bell dutifully rang. My charges bounced up and out the room on their way to lunch and connecting with friends.

All except one. A young man I'll call "Anthony" walked up to me at the front where I was sitting with the stack of quizzes.

You should know Anthony hadn't achieved an academic performance one would call "stellar" over the first two or three months of the semester, and that's putting it kindly. And since he wasn't particularly disciplined about his homework, he was missing the practice that normally gives students the confidence to perform well on the quizzes and tests I inflicted upon them.

"Hey, uh, Mr. Hurley."

"Hey, Anthony, what's up?"

"I, uh, was wondering. Um. Have you graded the quizzes yet?"

I glanced at the still-warm papers on the table next to me. "The quiz you just turned in? Not yet, but I'll do so later today so I can get it back to you tomorrow. How's that?"

"Er, could you, uh, could you grade it now?"

Something was clearly up.

"Hmmm … Okay, let's give it a look. I'll save the exact grade for later, but we can at least get a sense of how you did."

"Oh, thanks!"

I thumbed through the pages looking for his, hoping the heavens might have allowed this child some measure of success that he hadn't achieved up to that point in my class.

"Here it is. Let's see."

Looking down the page, there were remarkably few of the mistakes that normally congregated on his pages.

"Hey, this is pretty good! You made a few little errors here and there, but this is strong. I'd guess this is a B+ or perhaps even an A-. Great work!"

He broke into a mile-wide smile and blurted out an excited, "Yes! Yes! Wow!"

I grinned back. "Look at you!"

Unable to contain the secret, he enthusiastically let me in on his method. "Oh, Mr. Hurley. You know that studying thing? It really works!"

I made the wise decision of not following his comment with something I thought was funny.

Anyone who has ever worked with students has met those who, for whatever reason, hold themselves back from doing what they need to do. In fact, we all have those moments when we know what we should do, but then we hold back because we fear we won't succeed, or we are too comfortable, or we decide we're happy to let someone else take the lead.

As educators, time and time again, we give advice ("Ask yourself if you can do better," or "Have you had someone else give you feedback on that?" or similar) that, if followed, would result in small and profound improvements for us and our students—but do we act on our own words?

That is to ask, do we do what we should?

- Take the time to make a positive phone call to the parent of a student having difficulties.

- Give your students the chance to surprise you with their creativity by offering them a choice in how to approach a challenge.

- Learn every student's name as quickly as possible—they'll connect better with you when you bother to do so.

- Know the names of every adult you work with. The janitor you take time to chat with about the weather, sports, or music may very well have a useful idea when you need to try something unusual.

- Try a new tool or technique regularly. When you experiment, your students will become more comfortable pushing their ideas a little further.

- Have fun. While I would never say our job is to entertain students, sharing our enthusiasm for teaching can make our students want to come along for the ride, and perhaps realize that learning itself—discovering things, making connections, and seeing in themselves new possibilities—is a mountain of lifelong fun.

I know nothing I've said is new, and chances are good that you already know these things are important, but do you do them?

As Anthony would tell you, you should—"It really works."

Throughout the course of this book, I've attempted to paint a picture of what a school can become when we focus on fostering powerfully memorable learning experiences; when we share and build upon successes; when we regularly and collaboratively explore new possibilities; and when we realize that if we just put forth effort and develop confidence in ourselves and our students, we can all be something wonderfully *more*.

> If we just put forth effort and develop confidence in ourselves and our students, we can all be something wonderfully *more*.

I hope this book helps you have experiences that make it easy to respond if someone ever asks you, "What makes your school special?"

And finally, I hope you stay in touch.

A portion of the proceeds from this book will go to support the efforts of Next Vista for Learning,[1] my educational nonprofit. I invite you to explore and share the

---

[1] NextVista.org

site's library of videos celebrating creative teaching and learning everywhere.

I also encourage you to sign up for NextVista.org's monthly newsletter,[2] featuring new videos, contests, projects we're running, loads of freely available resources, and whatever else I think may inspire those of us who care about students.

I'll finish this book as I finish the newsletter each month, with this hope:

May you inspire, and be inspired, each and every day.

---

[2]   NextVista.org/newsletter

Thanks

There are hordes of folks to thank for anything in this book that may prove beneficial to others, so I'll take my best shot at acknowledging at least some of them.

(I am certain I am leaving out many who certainly deserve space here, so please forgive any omission as the kind of error common for one who has never learned how to keep a reasonable load on his plate.)

I thank the many colleagues and students who have taught me the joy and meaning of pursuing possibilities for others. Among them, special notes of appreciation go to Matt Hall, Wendy Ho, Rob Ly, Jerry Tolbert, Ken Bones, Ted Okano, Victor Zapata, Muriel Clack, Wes Roberts, and Jane Voss.

I thank Todd Seal, John Lozano, Darrell Shideler, Jeff Ota, and Andy Ratermann for the time they have devoted over the last decade to helping make NextVista. org a resource for teachers and students everywhere.

I thank my buddies and fellow explorers in the realm of educational technology, with special thanks for the heartfelt and ongoing encouragement of Gay Krause, Steve McGriff, Mike Lawrence, Ken Shelton, Mark Wagner, Monica Martinez, Jennie Magiera, Mark Dohn, Lisa Highfill, Diane Main, Nicole Dalesio, Gene Tognetti, Kim Randall, John Sowash, Jay Atwood, Hall Davidson, Steve Dembo, Dean Shareski, Adam Bellow, Leslie Fisher, Mark Allen, Steve Philp, Richard Knaggs, Ramsey Musallam, Darren Hudgins, Jeff Heil, Donnie Piercey, Kyle Pace, Andrew Schwab, Ben Rimes, Andy Losik, Jen Wagner, Cindy Lane, Bette Schneiderman, Mike Byrne, Steven Anderson, Tom Whitby, Kevin Brookhouser, Wes Roberts, Victor Zapata, Muriel Clack, Kyle and Elizabeth Brumbaugh, Jenn Womble, Corinne Takara, Meg Omainsky, Dennis Grice, Tammy Maginity, and Richard Byrne.

I thank Holly Clark of EdTechTeam for giving me the push I needed to make this book happen.

I thank my friends and colleagues at Junipero Serra High School, with special fist-bumps to Barry Thornton, Barb Luis, Gary Meegan, Kevin Carey, Ed Taylor, Rick Boesen, Peggy Farrell, Eric Plett, Mary Dowden, Laura Ramey, Ricardo Garcia, Alena Reyes, Sue Cordes, and Rita Lee.

I thank the many wonderful people at ISTE, FETC, MACUL, CUE, OETC, ASSET, and a dozen other organizations and conferences that have given me the chance to share ideas with and learn from thousands of amazing teachers.

I thank inspiring teachers like Dennis Plyler, Francis Conlon, Paula Cooey, Decker Walker, Hiroshi Sakamoto, and Don Clark for bringing joy, high expectations, and unforgettable insights to their classes. I am lucky to have been your student.

I thank the members of the Rotary eClub of Silicon Valley, as well as the other three Rotary clubs I've belonged to, for helping me understand the role service plays in our lives, tossing out a special thanks to Ursula and Barney Callaghan for setting the bar on hospitality.

I thank my brothers and sisters for teaching me how to be a better person, my father for teaching me to pursue opportunities, Mamaw for her faith and patience, Tetsuro and Junko Iseki for their friendship and kindness, Dale Whitman for being an uncle to me, all the Redmonds, Arnolds, Carrolls, Hurleys, and Rainwaters for the fun and caring that they bring to those lucky enough to know them, and everyone else in my family for their love and encouragement.

I thank my mother for living what it means to be a teacher. She has been sharing the joys of literature and writing with college students for more than forty years, enriching thousands of hearts and minds through her dedication.

Finally, I thank my wife for being the kind of friend every person hopes to have and the kind of love I believe is a gift of the heavens. Tabitha, I won life's lottery when I met you.

More Books from EdTechTeam Press
edtechteam.com/books

The HyperDoc Handbook
Digital Lesson Design Using Google Apps
By Lisa Highfill, Kelly Hilton, and Sarah Landis

The HyperDoc Handbook is a practical reference guide for all K–12 educators who want to transform their teaching into blended-learning environments. *The HyperDoc Handbook* is a bestselling book that strikes the perfect balance between pedagogy and how-to tips while also providing ready-to-use lesson plans to get you started with HyperDocs right away.

Innovate with iPad
Lessons to Transform Learning in the Classroom

By Karen Lirenman and Kristen Wideen

Written by two primary teachers, this book provides a complete selection of clearly explained, engaging, open-ended lessons to change the way you use iPad with students at home or in the classroom. It features downloadable task cards, student-created examples, and extension ideas to use with your students. Whether you have access to one iPad for your entire class or one for each student, these lessons will help you transform learning in your classroom.

The Space
A Guide for Educators

By Rebecca Louise Hare and Robert Dillon

The Space supports the conversation around revolution happening in education today concerning the reshaping of school spaces. This book goes well beyond the ideas for learning-space design th at focuses on Pinterest-perfect classrooms and instead discusses real and practical ways to design learning spaces that support and drive learning.

Classroom Management in the Digital Age
Effective Practices for Technology-Rich Learning Spaces

By Patrick Green and Heather Dowd

Classroom Management in the Digital Age helps guide and support teachers through the new landscape of device-rich classrooms. It provides practical strategies to novice and expert educators alike who want to maximize learning and minimize distraction. Learn how to keep up with the times while limiting time wasters and senseless screen-staring time.

The Google Apps Guidebook
Lessons, Activities, and Projects Created by Students for Teachers

By Kern Kelley and the Tech Sherpas

The Google Apps Guidebook is filled with great ideas for the classroom from the voice of the students themselves. Each chapter introduces an engaging project that teaches students (and teachers) how to use one of Google's powerful tools. Projects are differentiated for a variety of age ranges and can be adapted for most content areas.

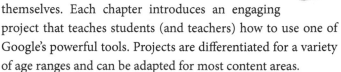

Code in Every Class
How All Educators Can Teach Programming

By Kevin Brookhouser and Ria Megnin

In *Code in Every Class*, Kevin Brookhouser and Ria Megnin explain why computer science is critical to your students' future success. With lesson ideas and step-by-step instruction, they show you how to take tech education into your own hands and open a world of opportunities to your students. And here's the best news: You *don't* have to be a computer genius to teach the basics of coding.

Making Your Teaching Something Special
50 Simple Ways to Become a Better Teacher

By Rushton Hurley

In the second book in his series, Rushton Hurley highlights key areas of teaching that play a part in shaping your success as an educator. Whether you are finding your way as a brand new teacher or are a seasoned teacher who is looking for some powerful ideas, this book offers inspiration and practical advice to help you make this year your best yet.

The Google Cardboard Book
Explore, Engage, and Educate with Virtual Reality

An EdTechTeam Collaboration

In *The Google Cardboard Book*, EdTechTeam trainers and leaders offer step-by-step instructions on how to use virtual reality technology in your classroom—no matter what subject you teach. You'll learn what tools you need (and how affordable they can be), which apps to start with, and how to view, capture, and share 360° videos and images.

Transforming Libraries
A Toolkit for Innovators, Makers, and Seekers

By Ron Starker

In the Digital Age, it's more important than ever
for libraries to evolve into gathering points for
collaboration, spaces for innovation, and places
where authentic learning occurs. In *Transforming Libraries*, Ron
Starker reveals ways to make libraries makerspaces, innovation
centers, community commons, and learning design studios that
engage multiple forms of intelligence.

Intention
Critical Creativity in the Classroom

By Amy Burvall and Dan Ryder

Inspiring and exploring creativity opens pathways
for students to use creative expression to demon-
strate content knowledge, critical thinking, and the
problem solving that will serve them best no matter what their
futures may bring. *Intention* offers a collection of ideas, activities, and reasons for bringing creativity to every lesson.

The Conference Companion
*Sketchnotes, Doodles, and Creative Play for
Teaching and Learning*

By Becky Green

Wherever you are learning, whatever your doodle
comfort level, this jovial notebook is your buddy.
Sketchnotes, doodles, and creative play await both you and your
students. Part workshop, part journal, and part sketchbook,
these simple and light-hearted scaffolds and lessons will transform your listening and learning experiences while providing
creative inspiration for your classroom.

Bring the World to Your Classroom
Using Google Geo Tools

By Kelly Kermode and Kim Randall

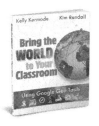

We live and work in a global society, but many students have only a very small community or neighborhood as their frame of reference. Expand their horizons and help them increase their understanding of how they fit in the global landscape using Google Geo Tools. This book is packed full of how-tos and sample projects to get you and your learners moving forward with mapping, exploring, and making connections to the world around you.

50 Ways to Use YouTube in the Classroom

By Patrick Green

Your students are already accessing YouTube, so why not meet them where they are as consumers of information? By using the tools they choose, you can maximize their understanding in ways that matter. *50 Ways to Use YouTube in the Classroom* is an accessible guide that will improve your teaching, your students' learning, and your classroom culture.

Illuminate
Technology Enhanced Learning

By Bethany Petty

In *Illuminate*, author, educator, and technology trainer Bethany Petty explains how to use technology to improve your students' learning experiences. You'll learn specific how-tos for using a wide variety of apps and tools as well as the why behind using technology. Meet your students' needs and make learning memorable using technology enhanced learning.

The Martians in Your Classroom
STEM in Every Learning Space

By Rachael Mann and Stephen Sandford

In *The Martians in Your Classroom*, educator Rachael Mann and former Director of Space Technology Exploration at NASA Stephen Sandford reveal the urgent need for science, technology, engineering, and math (STEM) and career and technical education (CTE) in every learning space. Proposing an international endeavor to stimulate students' interest in science and technology, they highlight the important roles educators, business leaders, and politicians can play in advancing STEM in schools.

More Now
A Message from the Future for the Educators of Today

By Mark Wagner, PhD

The priorities and processes of education must change if we are going to prepare students for their future. In *More Now*, EdTechTeam Founder Mark Wagner, explores the six essential elements of effective school change: courageous leaders, empowered teachers, student agency, inspiring spaces, robust infrastructure, and engaged communities. You'll learn from educational leaders, teachers, and technologists how you can make each of these essential elements part of your school or district culture—starting *now*.

40 Ways to Inject Creativity into Your Classroom with Adobe Spark

By Ben Forta and Monica Burns

Experienced educators Ben Forta and Monica Burns offer step-by-step guidance on how to incorporate this powerful tool into your classroom in ways that are meaningful and relevant. They present 40 fun and practical lesson plans suitable for a variety of ages and subjects as well as 15 graphic organizers to get you started. With the tips, suggestions, and encouragement in this book, you'll find everything you need to inject creativity into your classroom using Adobe Spark.

The Top 50 Chrome Extensions for the Classroom

By Christopher Craft, PhD

If you've ever wished there were a way to add more minutes to the day, Chrome Extensions just may be the answer. In *The Top 50 Chrome Extensions for the Classroom*, you'll learn time-saving tips and efficiency tricks that will help reduce the amount of time spent in lesson preparation and administrative tasks—so you can spend more time with students.

About The Author

Rushton Hurley is the founder and executive director of Next Vista for Learning (NextVista.org), which provides a free library of creative, educational videos by and for teachers and students. He has been a high school Japanese language teacher, a principal of an online school, a teacher trainer, an educational technology researcher, and a school reform consultant.

His graduate research at Stanford University included using speech recognition technology with beginning students of Japanese in computer-based role-playing scenarios for developing language skills. In the 1990s his work with teenagers at a high school in California led him to begin using internet and video technologies to make learning more active, helping him reach students who had struggled under more traditional approaches.

In 2005, Rushton began speaking at conferences to help teachers working to discover what digital media and other technologies could do for their classes. In the last decade, Rushton has trained teachers and other professionals in North America, Europe, Asia, and Africa, presenting at regional, national, and international conferences. His fun and thoughtful talks center on the connection between engaging learning and useful, affordable technology, as well as professional perspectives in an ever-changing world.

Made in the USA
Lexington, KY
16 August 2019